BTEC Level 3 National Study Skills Guide in Art and Design

Welcome to your Study Skills Guide! You can make it your own – start by adding your personal and course details below...

Learner's name: _____

BTEC course title: _____

Date started: _____

Mandatory units:

_____

_____

_____

Optional units:

_____

_____

_____

_____

Centre name: _____

Centre address:

_____

_____

_____

Tutor's name: _____

D0320511

Published by Pearson Education Limited, a company incorporated in England and Wales, having its registered office at Edinburgh Gate, Harlow, Essex, CM20 2JE. Registered company number: 872828

Edexcel is a registered trademark of Edexcel Limited

Text © Pearson Education Limited 2010

First published 2010

18   17

13   12

British Library Cataloguing in Publication Data

A catalogue record for this book is available from the British Library

ISBN 978 1 84690 564 3

Copyright notice

All rights reserved. No part of this publication may be reproduced in any form or by any means (including photocopying or storing it in any medium by electronic means and whether or not transiently or incidentally to some other use of this publication) without the written permission of the copyright owner, except in accordance with the provisions of the Copyright, Designs and Patents Act 1988 or under the terms of a licence issued by the Copyright Licensing Agency, Saffron House, 6–10 Kirby Street, London EC1N 8TS (www.cla.co.uk). Applications for the copyright owner's written permission should be addressed to the publisher.

Typeset and edited by DSM Partnership
Cover design by Visual Philosophy, created by eMC Design
Cover photo/illustration © SuperStock: Moodboard
Printed and bound L.E.G.O. S.p.A. Lavis (TN) - Italy

Acknowledgements

The publisher would like to thank the following for their kind permission to reproduce their photographs:

Alamy Images: Angela Hampton Picture Library 19, Claudia Wiens 66; Alan Parsons: 51, 51/2, 52, 52/2, 52/3, 52/4, 52/5, 52/6, 53, 53/2, 53/3; Corbis: 76; iStockphoto: 10, Mümin Inan 7, Chris Schmidt 33; Pearson Education Ltd: Steve Shott 28, Ian Wedgewood 59.

All other images © Pearson Education.

Every effort has been made to trace copyright holders of material reproduced in this book. Any omissions will be rectified in subsequent printings if notice is given to the publishers.

Websites

Go to www.pearsonhotlinks.co.uk to gain access to the relevant website links and information on how they can aid your studies. When you access the site, search for either the title BTEC Level 3 National Study Skills Guide in Art and Design or the ISBN 978184605643.

Disclaimer

This material has been published on behalf of Edexcel and offers high-quality support for the delivery of Edexcel qualifications.

This does not mean that the material is essential to achieve any Edexcel qualification, nor does it mean that it is the only suitable material available to support any Edexcel qualification. Edexcel material will not be used verbatim in setting any Edexcel examination or assessment. Any resource lists produced by Edexcel shall include this and other appropriate resources.

Copies of official specifications for all Edexcel qualifications may be found on the Edexcel website: www.edexcel.com

Contents

Popular progression pathways

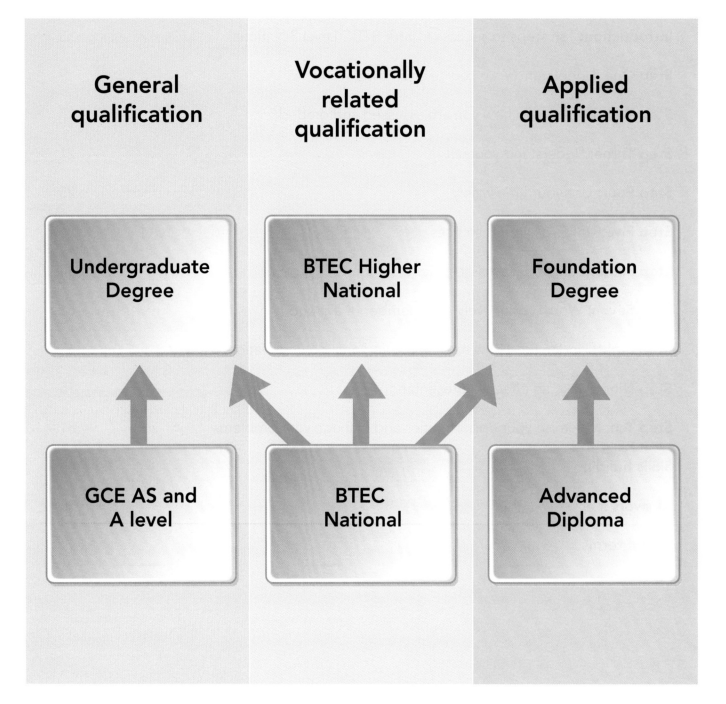

Ten steps to success in your BTEC Level 3 National

This Study Skills Guide has been written to help you achieve the best result possible on your BTEC Level 3 National course. At the start of a new course you may feel quite excited but also a little apprehensive. Taking a BTEC Level 3 National qualification has many benefits and is a major stepping-stone towards your future career. Using this Study Skills Guide will help you get the most out of your course from the start.

TOP TIP

Use this Study Skills Guide at your own pace. Dip in to find what you need. Look back at it whenever you have a problem or query.

During **induction** sessions at the start of your course, your tutor will explain important information, but it can be difficult to remember everything, and that's when you'll find this Study Skills Guide invaluable. Look at it whenever you want to check anything related to your course. It provides all the essential facts you need and has a Useful terms section to explain specialist terms, words and phrases, including some that you will see highlighted in this book in bold type.

This Study Skills Guide covers the skills you'll need to do well in your course – such as managing your time, researching and analysing information and preparing a presentation.

- Use the **Top tips** to make your life easier as you go.
- Use the **Key points** to help you to stay focused on the essentials.
- Use the **Action points** to check what you need to know or do now.
- Use the **Case studies** to relate information to your chosen sector and vocational area.

- Use the **Activities** to test your knowledge and skills.
- Use the **Useful terms** section to check the meaning of specialist terms.

This Study Skills Guide has been designed to work alongside the Edexcel Student Book for BTEC Level 3 National in Art and Design (Edexcel, 2010). This Student Book includes the main knowledge you'll need, with tips from BTEC experts, Edexcel assignment tips, assessment activities and up-to-date case studies from industry experts, plus handy references to your Study Skills Guide.

This Study Skills Guide is divided into ten steps, each relating to a key aspect of your studies, from understanding assessment to time management to maximising opportunities. Concentrate on getting things right one step at a time. Thousands of learners have achieved BTEC Level 3 National qualifications and are now studying for a degree or building a successful career at work. Using this Study Skills Guide, and believing in your own abilities, will help you achieve your future goals, too.

Introduction to the art and design sector

Art and design describes work which is creatively visual (art) and which has been created for a specific purpose (design). Some would say that art is for appreciation and design for function. Visual art and design covers:

2D work – drawing, painting, graphics, photography, printmaking

3D work – sculpture, architecture, interior design, product design/engineering, ceramics, jewellery, woven and printed textiles, glass, fashion

4D (also known as time-based) work – filmmaking, computer games, animation.

Your course will allow you to expand your creativity and gain a better understanding of art and design. You will undertake research, looking at both your work and the work of others, and analyse, evaluate and communicate your findings with growing skills, confidence and appreciation.

Your studies are constructed in such a way that the teaching and learning experience can prepare you for a general career in art and design. Alternatively you may want to develop more specialist skills, which will almost certainly involve further studies at degree and postgraduate levels. Specialist art and design pathways involve extended studies to develop new skills and competences at an accelerated level to meet the demands of industry, client needs and even students, if you decide to teach!

The BTEC Level 3 National in Art and Design provides a general grounding that will help you enhance your creative skills. You will develop technical and professional competencies that will equip you to investigate employment opportunities. If you decide to follow a specialist art and design pathway, there are options to progress to one of a vast range of higher-level courses in the creative sector that offer multidisciplinary study routes alongside specialist skills development.

A career in the creative industries is very hard work, but if you are able to succeed it will be worth all of the study. Working in the creative industries will give you the opportunity to work with other creative people; this might be in the world of fine art, the media, corporate design and advertising, industrial design, engineering, fashion and textiles, or theatre and television design. It can be very satisfying to see a piece of your own art, sculpture or photography in an exhibition or in print, or have someone buy your jewellery, ceramics or weaves. Working as part of a studio design team is also very exciting – there is the adrenalin of working to tight deadlines and the euphoria when the client is happy with the outcome, which makes the hard work totally worthwhile. However, in the creative industries you will also need to ensure that you are always up to date with current trends and aware of the development of other artists, both within your specialist area and beyond. Taking all the opportunities available on your BTEC Level 3 National course may help you to succeed.

You may work as part of a team of creative designers.

Skills for the art and design sector

Studying art and design requires a number of essential skills. Skills development is an ongoing process for every artist and designer who wants to expand their knowledge, increase their confidence and extend their ability.

As a student of art and design you should begin, from the outset, to study and practise as an artist or a designer, learning new skills in a creative context. Allow the essential skills to be a part of everyday activities, to inform and underpin every assignment and to influence the way you see things around you. You should always be seeking to record information and to investigate, experiment, communicate and evaluate.

These are some of the skills which you will develop on this course.

- Visual communication, through mark-making (two-dimensional (2D) design) and making (three-dimensional (3D) design).
- Contextual referencing, where you will learn about the work of other artists and designers.
- Exploration of creative ideas, where you will learn how to research and explore concepts that relate to a specific brief.
- Ideas development, where you will learn new creative and technical skills and methodology which allow you to progress initial design ideas.
- Presentation of your own and others' creative and technical proposals in individual and group work.

You will also be able to study optional (specialist) units of your choice depending on which pathway you have chosen to take. The optional units include Graphics for 3D Application, Location Photography, Fashion Styling, Exploring Specialist Textile Techniques, 3D Design Media, Techniques and Technology, Film and Video Editing Techniques, and Computer Game Design.

As a student of art and design you will learn in new and exciting ways, using contextual research (looking at the work of other artists and designers)

for influence and inspiration. You will learn new studio and workshop skills, such as visualising and working in two and three dimensions with mixed media, wood, metal and plastic.

Your studies will include gallery and exhibition visits and may involve travelling to different cities and countries to record (draw, photograph or film) subjects that interest and attract you and which may be of use in your current and future studies.

Here are some generic skills associated with art and design:

- investigation (through observation and research)
- recording (visual, spoken and written)
- experimentation (ideas development)
- communication (visual, spoken and written)
- analysis
- evaluation
- reflection.

Here are some specialist skills associated with art and design:

- 2D visual language
  - mark-making
  - sketching
  - conceptualising (drawing)
  - rendering
  - painting
  - image-making (photography, film)
- 3D visual language
  - cutting
  - joining
  - constructing
  - forming
  - modelling (maquettes and production).

Here are some formal elements – the language (used by artists, designers and craftspeople) associated with skills in art and design:

- line, tone, colour
- pattern, texture
- form, shape, scale, structure.

Art and design skills development is underpinned by the ability to receive, use and communicate information of all types. This could be:

- visual information
- written information
- digital information
- spoken information
- tactile information
- spatial information.

In art and design it is important to be able to self-direct and to measure your own abilities. This self-evaluation process involves making choices and electing to work with preferred techniques and specialist processes. These specialist choices need to be complemented by developing an awareness of all things creative, studying the work of others and developing responsive thought processes to new information and perceived opinions.

It is important to develop the ability to communicate through a three-stage process of research, ideas development and presentation. This will help you demonstrate a high level of creative art and design skills when working towards a specific goal. The design process may include additional activities between each stage, depending on the nature of the brief and the client requirements. Having three clear stages will assist you in making sure that you meet the assignment brief, keep to deadlines and ensure that your or your team's resources are in place. This will help you perform well in assignments.

The three stages are as follows:

Stage 1 involves analysis of the assignment or design brief, conducting appropriate research to create initial ideas.

Stage 2 involves analysis of the research, problem-solving and producing concepts to illustrate the development of initial ideas.

Stage 3 involves presenting solutions and may include an evaluation followed by amendments to the work as a result of criticism, feedback or comment during the presentation.

Your portfolio

All the skills that you use on this course will need to be evidenced through your portfolio. You will need to have a portfolio both on this course, in higher education and when you go out into the professional world.

Your portfolio should be made up of work from many different units to show the skills you have learned and to emphasise the range of your competences. It should obviously include work from your very strongest units, as well as the optional specialist units if you are going down a particular pathway.

Photographs of your work at various stages of completion can be included in your portfolio. This will be particularly useful if you produce something that is fragile, such as glass or a paper-based sculpture. Your sketchbooks will also provide good proof of how your ideas progress through a project.

Step One: Understand your course and how it works

Case study: Making decisions

Louise and George both enjoyed art at school but feel that they now want to experience a broader curriculum, which might help them to make decisions about higher education and possible careers in the creative industries.

They spoke with their art teacher, who explained that the BTEC Level 3 National would be an excellent study route as it offers a wide range of units and study experience. Louise and George are immediately attracted to this idea and want to know more. Their teacher suggests that they do some research into the course.

Louise and George also have some initial questions about the BTEC National in Art and Design and how it could work for them and their peers who are interested in creative studies. They decide to broaden their research to answer these questions as well.

They take their teacher's advice and start by compiling a list of places where they could find out about the further education experience, such as their learning resource centre and the college website, and by paying a visit to a local careers office. Their tutor has given them some good advice already, telling them to visit the Edexcel website to find out more about the

BTEC National qualifications and about those in Art and Design in particular.

Louise and George decide to invite their teacher to share in their findings by writing up a brief overview and by listing relevant bibliographical details and internet links .

Reflection points

Find out the answers to Louise's and George's questions.

- How will studying BTEC National in Art and Design open up employment and higher education opportunities?
- How long is the course, and are there more qualification options at the same level as the BTEC National?
- Who could advise you on the entry qualifications needed to be accepted on to the Level 3 qualification?
- Would somebody be able to study on a BTEC National and do part-time work at the same time so that they had some money to contribute towards their fees and materials?

All BTEC Level 3 National qualifications are **vocational** or **work-related**. This means that you gain specific knowledge and understanding relevant to your chosen area. It gives you several advantages when you start work. For example, you will already know quite a lot about your chosen area, which will help you settle down more quickly. If you are already employed, you become more valuable to your employer.

Your BTEC course will prepare you for the work you want to do.

There are four types of BTEC Level 3 National qualification:
Certificates, Subsidiary Diplomas, Diplomas and Extended Diplomas

	Certificate	Subsidiary Diploma	Diploma	Extended Diploma
Credit	30	60	120	180
Equivalence	1 AS level	1 A level	2 A levels	3 A levels

These qualifications are often described as **nested**. This means that they fit inside each other (rather like Russian dolls) because the same units are common to each qualification – so you can progress from one to another easily by completing more units.

TOP TIP

The structure of BTEC Level 3 National qualifications means it's easy to progress from one type to another and gain more credits, as well as to specialise in particular areas that interest you.

- Every BTEC Level 3 National qualification has a set number of **mandatory units** that all learners must complete.
- All BTEC Level 3 National qualifications include **optional units** that enable you to study particular areas in more depth.

- Some BTEC Level 3 National qualifications have **specialist pathways**, which may have additional mandatory units. These specialist pathways allow you to follow your career aims more precisely. For example, if you are studying to become an IT practitioner, you can choose pathways in software development, networking, systems support or IT and business.

- On all BTEC courses you are expected to be responsible for your own learning. Obviously your tutor will give you help and guidance when necessary, but you also need to be 'self-starting' and able to use your own initiative. Ideally, you can also assess how well you are doing and make improvements when necessary.

- BTEC Level 3 National grades convert to UCAS points, just like A-levels, but the way you are assessed and graded on a BTEC course is different, as you will see in the next section.

Key points

- You can study part-time or full-time for your BTEC Level 3 National.

- You can do a Certificate, Subsidiary Diploma, Diploma or Extended Diploma, and progress easily from one to the other.

- You will study both mandatory units and optional units on your course.

- When you have completed your BTEC course you can get a job (or **apprenticeship**), use your qualification to develop your career, and/or continue studying to degree level.

- On all BTEC Level 3 National courses, the majority of your learning is practical and vocationally focused to develop the skills you need for your chosen career.

Using the Edexcel website to find out about your course

- You can check all the details about your BTEC Level 3 National course on the Edexcel website – go to www.edexcel.com.

- Enter the title of your BTEC Level 3 National qualification in the qualifications finder.

- Now find the specification in the list of documents. This is a long document so don't try to print it. Instead, look at the information on the units you will be studying to see the main topics you will cover.

- Then save the document or bookmark the page so that you can easily refer to it again if you need to.

Action points

1 By discussing with your tutor and by exploring the Edexcel website, find out the key information about your course and use it to complete the 'Important information' form on the next page. You can refer to this form at any time to refresh your memory about any part of your studies.

a) Check whether you are studying for a BTEC Level 3 Certificate, Subsidiary Diploma, Diploma or Extended Diploma, and find out the number of units you will be studying.

b) Find out the titles of the mandatory units you will be studying.

c) Find out the titles of the optional units and identify the ones offered at your centre.

d) Check the length of your course, and when you will be studying each unit.

e) Identify the optional units you will be taking. On some National courses you will do this at the start, while on others you may make your final decision later.

f) Find out other relevant information about your BTEC Level 3 National qualification. Your centre may have already given you details about the course structure.

g) Ask your tutor to help you to complete section 10 on the form. Depending on your course, you may be developing specific additional or personal skills – such as personal, learning and thinking skills (PLTS) and functional skills – or spending time on work experience, going on visits, or doing other activities linked to your subject area.

h) Talk to your tutor about section 12 on the form, as your sources of information will depend on the careers guidance and information at your centre. You may find it useful to exchange ideas with other members of your class.

IMPORTANT INFORMATION ON MY BTEC LEVEL 3 NATIONAL COURSE	
1	The title of the BTEC Level 3 National qualification I am studying is:
2	The length of my course is:
3	The total number of units I will study is:
4	The number of mandatory units I have to study is:
5	The titles of these mandatory units and the dates (or terms) when I will study them are:
6	The main topics I will learn in each mandatory unit include:

IMPORTANT INFORMATION ON MY BTEC LEVEL 3 NATIONAL COURSE	
7	The number of optional units I have to study is:
8	The titles of the optional units I will study are:
9	The main topics I will learn in each optional unit include:
10	Other important aspects of my course are:
11	After I have achieved my BTEC Level 3 National my options include:
12	Useful sources of information I can use to find out more about these options include:

2 Many learners already have information, contacts or direct experience that relate to their course. For example, you may have a specific interest or hobby that links to a unit, such as being a St John Ambulance cadet if you are studying Public Services. Think about the relevant sources of information you already have access to and complete the table below.

MY INFORMATION SOURCES	
Experts I know	(Who they are, what they know)
My hobbies and interests	(What they are, what they involve)
My job(s)	(Past and present work and work experience, and what I did)
Programmes I like to watch	(What these are, how they relate to my course)
Magazines and/or books I read	(What these are, examples of relevant articles)
ICT sources	(My centre's intranet as well as useful websites)
Other	(Other sources relevant for my particular course and the topics I will be studying)

Activity: Your future options

At the beginning of a new course it is helpful to think about what options may be available to you for your career and for a possible pathway into the art and design workforce. All assignments on the programme contribute to your final grade, and knowing what you are aiming for will help keep you motivated.

Using a mind map to explore different ideas is a way for you to start to consider the range of options available to you and to start investigating what you will need to follow each career pathway.

For example, if you wish to use visual communication skills in your work, you could explore the different routes to becoming a graphic designer.

You will find the internet a useful source of information. You could start by looking at websites such as madjobs (Marketing Advertising and Design jobs). Go to page 96 for details of how to access this website.

Make a list of the types of jobs you might be interested in. Use the table on the next page to create your list, along with notes about the skills required to do each job.

TOP TIP

People usually perform better if they understand why they have chosen, or been asked, to do something.

Job types and skills required

Job type	Skills required

Step Two: Understand how you are assessed and graded

Case study: Assignments and grading

During his induction week for the BTEC National in Art and Design, Jamie had been provided with information on the BTEC National qualification. The information was reasonably straightforward, but Jamie reckons that the assessment process is going to be very different to what he has been used to during secondary school. He is reading information about 'formative and summative assessment', about being assessed against 'unit grading criteria' and being graded with pass, merit or distinction rather than marks and percentages.

Jamie's tutor has announced that he is running an assessment and grading forum at the end of the induction week. He reassures Jamie and his friends that a group discussion (the forum) is going to prove a very useful and will help them understand how they will be assessed and what they will be assessed on.

The tutor suggests that a sample assignment (see page 41 in this guide) should be reviewed in tandem with the assessment and grading guidance. The assignment has been written to a standard format, which will be used for every brief on the BTEC National in Art and Design course regardless of whether it is a brief for graphics, 3D, fine art, textiles or another specialism.

Jamie and his friends are given a questionnaire, which they should bring to the assessment and grading forum. Their tutor advises that all questions will be answered during the event, but that they should prepare for the Q&A activity in advance by reading the information they have been given and looking through the sample assignment brief.

Jamie wants to ask these questions.

1 What is assessment and grading?
2 How often will assessment and grading take place?
3 Who will carry out assessment and grading?
4 Will my grading have a currency in higher education and employment?

Reflection point

Do you know the answers to Jamie's questions?

Your assessment

This section looks at the importance of your assignments, how they are graded, and how this converts into unit points and UCAS points. Unlike A-levels, there are no externally-set final exams on a BTEC course. Even if you know this because you already have a BTEC First qualification, you should still read this section, as now you will be working at a different level.

Your learning is assessed by **assignments** set by your tutors. You will complete these throughout your course, using many different **assessment methods**, such as real-life case studies, **projects** and presentations. Some assignments may be work-based or **time-constrained** – it depends very much on the vocational area you are studying.

Your assignments are based on **learning outcomes** set by Edexcel. These are listed for each unit in your course specification. You must achieve **all** the learning outcomes to pass each unit.

TOP TIP

Check the learning outcomes for each unit by referring to the course specification – go to www.edexcel.com.

Important skills to help you achieve your grades include:

- researching and analysing information (see page 63)
- using your time effectively (see page 25)
- working co-operatively as a member of a team (see page 57).

Your grades, unit points and UCAS points

On a BTEC Level 3 National course, assessments that meet the learning outcomes are graded as pass, merit or distinction. The different grades within each unit are set out by Edexcel as **grading criteria** in a **grading grid**. These criteria identify the **higher-level skills** you must demonstrate

to achieve a higher grade (see also Step Six: Understand your assessment, on page 35).

All your assessment grades earn **unit points**. The total points you get for all your units determines your final qualification grade(s) – pass, merit or distinction. You get:

- one final grade if you are taking a Certificate or Subsidiary Diploma
- two final grades if you are taking a Diploma
- three final grades if you are taking an Extended Diploma.

Your points and overall grade(s) convert to **UCAS points**, which you need to be accepted onto a degree course. For example, if you achieve three final pass grades for your BTEC Level 3 Extended Diploma, you get 120 UCAS Tariff points. If you achieve three final distinction grades, this increases to 360 – equivalent to three GCE A-levels.

Please note that all UCAS information was correct at the time of going to print, but we would advise that you check the UCAS website for the most up-to-date information. See page 96 for how to access their website.

Case study: Securing a university place

Chris and Shaheeda both want a university place and have worked hard on their BTEC Level 3 Extended Diploma course.

Chris's final score is 226 unit points, which converts to 280 UCAS Tariff points. Shaheeda has a total score of 228 unit points – just two points more – which converts to 320 UCAS points! This is because a score of between 204

and 227 unit points gives 280 UCAS points, whereas a score of 228 to 251 points gives 320 UCAS points.

Shaheeda is delighted because this increases her chances of getting a place on the degree course she wants. Chris is annoyed. He says if he had realised, he would have worked harder on his last assignment to get two more points.

You start to earn points from your first assessment, so you get many benefits from settling in quickly and doing good work from the start. Understanding how **grade boundaries** work also helps you to focus your efforts to get the best possible final grade.

You will be able to discuss your learning experiences, your personal progress and the

achievement of your learning objectives in **individual tutorials** with your tutor. These enable you to monitor your progress and overcome temporary difficulties. You can also talk about any worries you have. Your tutor is one of your most important resources, and a tutorial gives you their undivided attention.

You can talk through any questions or problems in your tutorials.

Key points

- Your learning is assessed in a variety of ways, such as by assignments, projects and real-life case studies.
- You need to demonstrate specific knowledge and skills to achieve the learning outcomes set by Edexcel. You must achieve all the grading criteria to pass a unit.
- The grading criteria for pass, merit and distinction are shown in a grading grid for the unit. Higher-level skills are needed for higher grades.
- The assessment grades of pass, merit and distinction convert to unit points. The total unit points you receive for the course determine your final overall grade(s) and UCAS points.

TOP TIP

It's always tempting to spend longer on work you like doing and are good at, but focusing on improving your weak areas will do more to boost your overall grade(s).

Action points

1 Find out more about your own course by carrying out this activity.

a) Find the learning outcomes for the units you are currently studying. Your tutor may have given you these, or you can find them in your course specification – go to www.edexcel.com.

b) Look at the grading grid for the units and identify the way the requirements change for the higher grades. If there are some unfamiliar words, check these in Step Six of this guide (see page 35 onwards).

c) If the unit points system still seems complicated, ask your tutor to explain it.

d) Check the UCAS points you would need for the course or university which interests you.

e) Design a form you can use to record the unit points you earn throughout your course. Keep this up to date. Regularly check how your points relate to your overall grade(s), based on the grade boundaries for your qualification. Your tutor can give you this information, or you can check it yourself in the course specification.

Activity: Understanding your course

Take a current BTEC National Art and Design assignment brief, which can be from any unit or integrated unit assignment. Read through the scheme of work carefully and review your assigned tasks and try to draft some answers to the questions below. Do not worry if you cannot answer all of the questions – your course tutors and assessors are there to guide you!

1 Name two types of assessment for BTEC qualifications.

2 What are unit assessment grading criteria?

3 Describe two ways which staff will use to tell me if I am making progress.

4 If necessary, will I be able to improve my assessment grades during my course? If so, how?

5 If I am unhappy with my assessment grades can I appeal? If so, how?

6 Name two opportunities for gathering assessment evidence on a BTEC Level 3 National in Art and Design course (for example, presenting your work to your class).

Step Three: Understand yourself

Case study: Being self-aware

Understanding yourself is essential in progressing your skills and abilities. Developing self-awareness and identifying preferences builds confidence and conviction. Art and design is hugely subjective, and self-promotion is an indispensable skill that underpins success in study and future employment.

To help some Level 3 learners develop their self-perception, their course tutor gave them a list of generic topics and asked them to try to relate the issues raised by these topics to what they knew about themselves.

- **Motivation** – Do I really want to learn? Do I really want to spend more time studying?
- **Study route** – What makes me want to study art and design?
- **Employment route** – Will I find work in the competitive creative industries?
- **Work ethic** – What will I do if I do not get work straight away?

- **Transferable skills** – Will any aspect of my specialist (art and design) studies provide me with transferable skills?

The learners chatted amongst themselves and then each came up with their own questions for the tutor about key aspects of self-awareness in the context of BTEC National studies.

Many raised the same issues, and these questions came up more than once:

- How will I develop new skills and abilities on a Level 3 BTEC National Art and Design course?
- How will these new skills and abilities develop my career potential?
- How can I measure my strengths and weaknesses in the direct context of taking a BTEC National Art and Design course?

Reflection point

Do you know the answers to these questions? If not, you could ask your tutor.

Self-awareness means understanding how you 'tick'. For example, do you prefer practical activities rather than theory? Do you prefer to draw or sketch an idea, rather than write about it?

Self-awareness is important as it makes you less reliant on other people's opinions and gives you confidence in your own judgement. You can also reflect on your actions to learn from your experiences.

Self-awareness also means knowing your own strengths and weaknesses. Knowing your strengths enables you to feel positive and confident about yourself and your abilities. Knowing your weaknesses means you know the areas you need to develop.

You can analyse yourself by looking at...

... your personality and preferences

You may have taken a personality test at your centre. If not, your tutor may recommend one to use, or there are many available online.

Many employers ask job candidates to complete a personality test so that they can match the type of work they are offering to the most suitable people. Although these tests can only give a broad indication of someone's personality, they may help to avoid mismatches, such as hiring someone who is introverted to work in sales.

... your skills and abilities

To succeed in your assignments, and to progress in a career, require a number of skills. Some may be vocationally-specific, or professional, skills that you can improve during your course – such as sporting performance on a Sports course. Others are broader skills that are invaluable no matter what you are studying – such as communicating clearly and co-operating with others.

You will work faster and more accurately, and have greater confidence, if you are skilled and proficient. A quick skills check will identify any problem areas.

TOP TIP

Use the Skills building section on page 85 to identify the skills you need for your course. You'll also find hints and tips for improving any weak areas.

Key points

- You need certain skills and abilities to get the most out of your BTEC Level 3 National course and to develop your career potential.

- Knowing your strengths and weaknesses is a sign of maturity. It gives you greater confidence in your abilities and enables you to focus on areas for improvement.

TOP TIP

You will find more help in this guide on developing your skills in using time wisely (Step Four), working as a member of a group (Step Seven), researching and analysing information (Step Eight) and making effective presentations (Step Nine).

Action points

1 Gain insight into your own personality by ticking **True** or **False** against each of the following statements. Be honest!

		True	False
a)	If someone annoys me, I can tell them about it without causing offence.		
b)	If someone is talking, I often interrupt them to give them my opinion.		
c)	I get really stressed if I'm under pressure.		
d)	I can sometimes become very emotional and upset on other people's behalf.		
e)	I sometimes worry that I can't cope and may make a mess of something.		
f)	I am usually keen, enthusiastic and motivated to do well.		
g)	I enjoy planning and organising my work.		
h)	I find it easy to work and co-operate with other people and take account of their opinions.		
i)	I am easily influenced by other people.		
j)	I often jump to conclusions and judge people and situations on first impressions.		
k)	I prefer to rely on facts and experience rather than following my instincts.		

Now identify which of the skills and qualities in the box below will be really important in your chosen career.

> **tact** **truthfulness** **listening skills**
>
> **staying calm under pressure**
>
> **empathy with others** **self-confidence**
>
> **initiative** **planning and organising**
>
> **working with others** **self-assurance**
>
> **objective judgements**

Use your answers to identify areas you should work on to be successful in the future.

2 As part of the UCAS process, all **higher education** applicants have to write a personal statement. This is different from a CV, which is a summary of achievements that all job applicants prepare. You may have already prepared a CV but not thought about a personal statement. Now is your chance!

Read the information about personal statements in the box. Then answer these questions:

a) Explain why personal statements are so important for higher education applicants.

b) Why do you think it is important for your personal statement to read well and be error-free?

c) Suggest three reasons why you shouldn't copy a pre-written statement you have found online.

d) Look at some websites to see what to include in the statement and how to set it out.

e) Prepare a bullet point list of ten personal facts. Focus on your strengths and on good reasons why you should be given a place on the higher education course of your choice. If possible, discuss your list with your tutor. Then keep it safe, as it will be useful if you need to write a personal statement later.

Personal statements

This is the information that all higher education applicants have to put in the blank space on their UCAS form. The aim is to sell yourself to admissions tutors. It can be pretty scary, especially if you haven't written anything like it before.

So, where do you start?

First, *never* copy pre-written statements you find online. These are just for guidance. Even worse are websites that offer to write your statement for a fee, and send you a few general, pre-written paragraphs. Forget them all: you can do better!

Imagine you are an admissions tutor with 60 places to offer to 200 applicants. What will you need to read in a personal statement to persuade you to offer the applicant a place?

Most likely, clear explanations about:

- what the applicant can contribute to the course

- why the applicant really wants a place on your course

- what the applicant has done to further his/her own interests in this area, such as voluntary work

- attributes that show this applicant would be a definite bonus – such as innovative ideas, with evidence eg 'I organised a newsletter which we published every three months …'

A personal statement should be well written, with no grammatical or spelling errors, and organised into clear paragraphs.

For further guidance on personal statements, go to page 96 to find out how to access a number of helpful websites.

Activity: Reviews and evaluations

In this activity you will design a simple way of helping you to review and evaluate your own work. This is an essential study skill, and you will need to go through this process when studying any BTEC National Art and Design unit. You will be graded on your capacity to be critical about your own work, and this activity will help you provide evidence to show that you are capable of self-evaluation.

Think about the way you normally set about doing an art assignment. What do you like to do first? Do you sketch something or do you go straight into drawing? Do you have all materials to hand and prepared before you start, or do you work more creatively if you haven't got the materials organised? If you think clearly about the way that you work and organise yourself, this will make it easier to evaluate yourself and to think about whether the way that you work poses any risks.

Here are the key words for any evaluation processs:

- reflect
- revise
- question
- analyse.

They are given in no particular order, but they are key to understanding how to develop creative ideas.

Put the key words in the boxes (one per box) in such a way that you establish a logical evaluation process. To what extent do you think that evaluation is continuous?

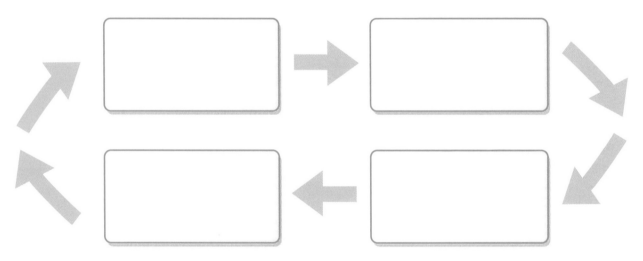

Use this process to help you to design a diagram of how you could work to support your own progress. Keep a copy in your file. You could then use this as evidence of how you undertake self-evaluation.

Step Four: Use your time wisely

 Case study: Time management

Some BTEC National in Art and Design learners have received their first major brief. This has a six-week timeline. Jonathan is initially quite relieved, as are his friends, that there is so much time before the deadline.

However, when he reads the assignment in more detail he finds that there are quite a few activities that have to be undertaken to produce the mandatory evidence – and, as Jonathan comments, the 'mandate' is just to meet the pass criteria.

The assignment brief concluded with a bold caption: **Time management is the linchpin to meeting the deadline.**

As well as the final deadline, dates for interim assessment points are also given in the brief. After the initial euphoria of looking at six weeks to complete his assignment, Jonathan quickly realises that the brief requires him to use his time wisely.

Using different-coloured highlighters, he marks the brief so he can clearly distinguish the:

- activities
- interim assessment dates
- presentation
- final deadline.

Then he uses the brief to set himself a series of questions which he intends to research to help him to use the next six weeks wisely.

- How can I organise my time to be more productive?
- How can I learn to prioritise assigned tasks?
- How can I avoid time-wasters in a team-based project?

Reflection points

How good are you at organising your time?

How could you improve your time management?

Most learners have to combine course commitments with other responsibilities such as a job (either full-time or part-time) and family responsibilities. You will also want to see your friends and keep up your hobbies and interests. Juggling these successfully means you need to be able to use your time wisely.

This involves planning what to do and when to do it to prevent panics about unexpected deadlines. As your course progresses, this becomes even more important, as your workload may increase towards the end of a term. In some cases, there could be two or more assignments to complete simultaneously. Although tutors try to avoid clashes of this sort, it is sometimes inevitable.

To cope successfully you need time-management skills, in particular:

- how to organise your time to be more productive
- how to prioritise tasks
- how to overcome time-wasters.

Organising your time

- **Use a diary or wall chart.**
  Using a different colour pen for each, enter:
  - your course commitments, such as assignment dates, tutorials, visits
  - important personal commitments, such as sports matches, family birthdays
  - your work commitments.

TOP TIP

A diary is useful because you can update it as you go, but a wall chart gives you a better overview of your commitments over several weeks. Keep your diary or chart up to date, and check ahead regularly so that you have prior warning of important dates.

- **Identify how you currently use your time.**
  - Work out how much time you spend at your centre, at work, at home and on social activities.
  - Identify which commitments are vital and which are optional, so you can find extra time if necessary.
- **Plan and schedule future commitments.**
  - Write down any appointments and tasks you must do.
  - Enter assignment review dates and final deadline dates in different colours.
  - This should stop you from arranging a dental appointment on the same morning that you are due to give an important presentation – or planning a hectic social life when you have lots of course work to do.

- **Decide your best times for doing course work.**
  - Expect to do most of your course work in your own time.
  - Work at the time of day when you feel at your best.
  - Work regularly, and in relatively short bursts, rather than once or twice a week for very long stretches.
  - If you're a night owl, allow an hour to 'switch off' before you go to bed.
- **Decide where to work.**
  - Choose somewhere you can concentrate without interruption.
  - Make sure there is space for resources you use, such as books or specialist equipment.
  - You also need good lighting and a good – but not too comfortable – chair.
  - If you can't find suitable space at home, check out your local or college library.
- **Assemble the items you need.**
  - Book ahead to get specific books, journals or DVDs from the library.
  - Ensure you have your notes, handouts and assignment brief with you.
  - Use sticky notes to mark important pages in textbooks or folders.

TOP TIP

Set yourself a target when you start work, so that you feel positive and productive at the end. Always try to end a session when a task is going well, rather than when you are stuck. Then you will be keener to go back to it the next day. Note down outstanding tasks you need to continue with next time.

- **Plan ahead.**
  - If anything is unclear about an assignment, ask your tutor for an explanation as soon as you can.
  - Break down assignments into manageable chunks, such as: find information, decide what to use, create a plan for finished work, write rough draft of first section etc.
  - Work back from deadline dates so that you allow plenty of time to do the work.
  - Always allow more time than you need. It is better to finish early than to run out of time.

TOP TIP

If you are working on a task as a group, organise and agree times to work together. Make sure you have somewhere to meet where you can work without disturbing other courses or groups.

- **Be self-disciplined.**
  - Don't put things off because you're not in the mood. Make it easier by doing simple tasks first to get a sense of achievement. Then move on to something harder.
  - Plan regular breaks. If you're working hard, you need a change of activity to recharge your batteries.
  - If you have a serious problem or personal crisis, talk to your personal tutor promptly.

TOP TIP

Make sure you know the consequences of missing an assignment deadline, as well as the dispensations and exemptions that can be given if you have an unavoidable and serious problem, such as illness (see also page 36).

How to prioritise tasks

Prioritising means doing the most important and urgent task first. Normally this will be the task or assignment with the closest deadline or the one that will most affect your overall course grades.

One way of prioritising is to group tasks into ABC categories.

Category A tasks	These must be done now as they are very important and cannot be delayed, such as completing an assignment to be handed in tomorrow.
Category B tasks	These are jobs you should do if you have time, because otherwise they will rapidly become Category A, such as getting a book that you need for your next assignment.
Category C tasks	These are tasks you should do if you have the time, such as rewriting notes jotted down quickly in a lesson.

Expect to be flexible. For example, if you need to allow time for information to arrive, then send for this first. If you are working in a team, take into account other people's schedules when you are making arrangements.

Avoiding time-wasters

Everyone has days when they don't know where the time has gone. It may be because they were constantly interrupted or because things just kept going wrong. Whatever the reason, the end result is that some jobs don't get done.

If this happens to you regularly, you need to take steps to keep on track. Here are some useful tips.

- **Warn people in advance when you will be working.**
  - Ask them to not interrupt you.
  - If you are in a separate room, shut the door. If someone comes in, make it clear you don't want to talk.
  - If that doesn't work, find somewhere else (or some other time) to work.
- **Switch off your mobile, the television and radio, and your iPod/MP3 player.**
  - Don't respond to, or make, calls or texts.
  - If someone rings your home phone, let voicemail answer or ask them to call back later.
- **Be strict with yourself when you are working online.**
  - Don't check your email until you've finished work.
  - Don't get distracted when searching for information.
  - Keep away from social networking sites.
- **Avoid displacement activities.**
  - These are the normally tedious jobs, such as cleaning your computer screen, that suddenly seem far more attractive than working!

Talking to friends can occupy a lot of time.

TOP TIP

The first step in managing your own time is learning to say 'no' (nicely!) if someone asks you to do something tempting when you should be working.

Key points

- Being in control of your time allows you to balance your commitments according to their importance and means you won't let anyone down.
- Organising yourself and your time involves knowing how you spend your time now, planning when and where it is best to work, scheduling commitments and setting sensible timescales to complete your work.
- Knowing how to prioritise means you will schedule work effectively according to its urgency and importance. You will need self-discipline to follow the schedule you have set for yourself.
- Identifying ways in which you may waste time means you can guard against these to achieve your goals more easily.

TOP TIP

Benefits to managing your own time include being less stressed (because you are not reacting to problems or crises), producing better work and having time for a social life.

Action points

1 Start planning your time properly.

a) Find out how many assignments you will have this term, and when you will get them. Put this information into your diary or planner.

b) Update this with your other commitments for the term – both work-/course-related and social. Identify possible clashes and decide how to resolve the problem.

c) Identify one major task or assignment you will do soon. Divide it into manageable chunks and decide how long to allow for each chunk, plus some spare time for any problems. If possible, check your ideas with your tutor before you put them into your planner.

2 How good are you at being responsible for your own learning?

a) Fill in this table. Score yourself out of 5 for each area, where 0 is awful and 5 is excellent. Ask a friend or relative to score you as well. See if you can explain any differences.

	Scoring yourself	Other person's score for you
Being punctual		
Organisational ability		
Tidiness		
Working accurately		
Finding and correcting own mistakes		
Solving problems		
Accepting responsibility		
Working with details		
Planning how to do a job		
Using own initiative		
Thinking up new ideas		
Meeting deadlines		

b) Draw up your own action plan for areas where you need to improve. If possible, talk this through at your next **tutorial** (see page 18).

Activity: Planning your time

Using time wisely is an excellent skill. Devise a flow diagram in the space below to demonstrate how you would practise time management on a specific project. Elements that you could focus on include:

- tasks
- evidence
- deadlines
- resources
- research
- ideas development
- design development
- presentation
- analysis
- evaluation.

Using your flow diagram, apply timelines to specific project tasks. You will soon realise the benefits of good time management. Your flow diagram can be used as assessment evidence and may also be a useful reference for other projects. Go to page 96 to find out how to access websites containing useful information about time management and organising projects.

Step Five: Utilise all your resources

Case study: Approaching new projects

Starting a new project generates mixed emotions, and Emily, Nihal and Jacinder, learners on a BTEC National Art and Design course, are no exception to this rule.

With the rest of their class, they are anticipating the assignment brief with some anxiety. After discussing their feelings, the three friends find they share the same concerns and thoughts.

- Will I enjoy the assignment?
- Will I understand the brief?
- Will the ideas flow?
- Will I present my ideas clearly?
- Will I be able to develop my ideas?
- Will I present my work to a good standard?
- Will I meet the deadline?
- Will I meet the assessment criteria?

The course tutor explains that making good use of available resources is the key to successful project outcomes and achieving the higher grades. She provides a whiteboard diagram to identify the main resources available to the BTEC National, listing both generic and subject-specific components.

The tutor also has some questions for the group in relation to storage and information retrieval.

How can digital information be best stored for easy retrieval?

How can handouts be filed for easy referencing?

How can visual work be recorded and stored so it is easily available?

Reflection point

Think about how you would answer these questions.

Your resources are all the things that can help you to be successful in your BTEC Level 3 National qualification, from your favourite website to your **study buddy** (see page 32) who collects handouts for you if you miss a class.

Your centre will provide essential resources, such as a library with appropriate books and electronic reference sources, the computer network and internet access. You will have to provide basic resources such as pens, pencils and file folders yourself. If you have to buy your own textbooks, look after them carefully so you can sell them on at the end of your course.

Here is a list of resources, with tips for getting the best out of them.

- **Course information**. This includes your course specification, this Study Skills Guide and all information on the Edexcel website relating to your BTEC Level 3 National course. Course information from your centre will include term dates, assignment dates and your timetable. Keep everything safely so you can refer to it whenever you need to clarify something.

- **Course materials**. These include course handouts, printouts and your own notes and textbooks. Put handouts into an A4 folder as soon as you get them. Use a separate folder for each unit you study.

TOP TIP

Filing notes and handouts promptly means they don't get lost and will stay clean and uncrumpled, and you won't waste time looking for them.

- **Stationery**. You need pens and pencils, a notepad, a hole puncher, a stapler and sets of dividers. Dividers should be clearly labelled to help you store and quickly find notes, printouts and handouts. Your notes should be headed and dated, and those from your own research must also include your source (see Step Eight, page 63 onwards.)

- **People**. Your tutors, specialist staff at college, classmates, your employer and work colleagues, and your relatives and friends are all valuable resources. Many will have particular skills or work in the vocational area that you are studying. Talking to other learners can help to clarify issues that there may not have been time to discuss fully in class.

A **study buddy** is another useful resource as they can make notes and collect handouts if you miss a session. (Remember to return the favour when they are away.)

Always be polite when you are asking people for information. Prepare the questions first and remember that you are asking for help, not trying to get them to do the work for you! If you are interviewing someone for an assignment or project, good preparations are vital. (See Step Eight, page 63 onwards.)

If someone who did the course before you offers help, be careful. It is likely the course requirements will have changed. Never be tempted to copy their assignments (or someone else's). This is **plagiarism** – a deadly sin in the educational world (see also Step Six, page 36.)

TOP TIP

A positive attitude, an enquiring mind and the ability to focus on what is important will have a major impact on your final result.

Key points

- Resources help you to achieve your qualification. Find out what resources you have available to you and use them wisely.

- Have your own stationery items.

- Know how to use central facilities and resources such as the library, learning resource centres and your computer network. Always keep to the policy on IT use in your centre.

- People are a key resource – school or college staff, work colleagues, members of your class, friends, family and people who are experts in their field.

Action points

1 a) List the resources you will need to complete your course successfully. Identify which ones will be provided by your school or college, and which you need to supply yourself.

b) Go through your list again and identify the resources you already have (or know how to access) and those you don't.

c) Compare your list with a friend's and decide how to obtain and access the resources you need. Add any items to your list that you forgot.

d) List the items you still need to get, and set a target date for doing this.

2 'Study buddy' schemes operate in many centres. Find out if this applies to your own centre and how you can make the best use of it.

In some you can choose your study buddy, in others people are paired up by their tutor.

- Being a study buddy might mean just collecting handouts when the other person is absent, and giving them important news.

- It may also mean studying together and meeting (or keeping in contact by phone or email) to exchange ideas and share resources.

With a study buddy you can share resources and stay on top of the course if you're ever away.

Activity: Resources

There are many resources that are available to all, often free of charge, and usually easily accessible. Tutors will always provide you with resource guidance, and there are key sources of information in school or college. However, it is useful to develop your own personal list of resources that you can use as the basis for personal progress and specialist skills development. Remember that this list will constantly expand as the course progresses, so it may be worth keeping an electronic list that can be easily updated.

Start your list by trying to complete the table below with some previous, current and newly-discovered resources. You could create a similar table electronically.

Libraries	
Galleries	
Books, periodicals, journals and articles	
Online bibliographies and other electronic resources	

Step Six: Understand your assessment

Case study: Assignment queries

Dean's course have been given an assignment brief consisting of three separate projects structured to meet outcomes relating to one of the core units on his BTEC National in Art and Design. During a briefing in class, his tutor explains that assignments are a way of producing assessment evidence, and often involve a range of activities that will generate evidence to meet the unit grading criteria.

The tutor goes on to explain that if learners are to meet the required generic and specialist standards, they need:

- familiarity with BTEC National assessment and grading criteria (pass, merit and distinction)
- an understanding of the assignment in the context of specific BTEC National Art and Design unit assessment criteria
- an understanding of the basic assessment criteria for a pass in the context of the scheme of work for the assignment tasks

- to investigate the potential to deliver evidence that goes beyond the pass criteria and to respond positively to key grading descriptors.

Reflection points

Dean has several questions he wants to check out with his tutor after reading his assignment brief carefully. Think about whether you can answer these questions in relation to your own course.

Does my college have an assessment policy document? How does it apply to me?

Will I find information about BTEC assessment policies on the Edexcel website?

Will I find the grading criteria for BTEC National Art and Design Units in my course specification?

How can I find out about how I can achieve merit and distinction grades?

Being successful on any BTEC Level 3 National course means first understanding what you must do in your assignments – and then doing it.

Your assignments focus on topics you have already covered in class. If you've attended regularly, you should be able to complete them confidently.

However, there are some common pitfalls it's worth thinking about. Here are tips to avoid them:

- Read the instructions (the assignment brief) properly and several times before you start.
- Make sure you understand what you are supposed to do. Ask if anything is unclear.

- Complete every part of a task. If you ignore a question, you can't meet the grading criteria.
- Prepare properly. Do your research or reading before you start. Don't guess the answers.
- Communicate your ideas clearly. You can check this by asking someone who doesn't know the subject to look at your work.
- Only include relevant information. Padding out answers makes it look as if you don't know your subject.
- Do the work earlier rather than later to avoid any last-minute panics.
- Pay attention to advice and feedback that your tutor has given you.

TOP TIP

Most learners don't do their best in assessments because of silly mistakes, carelessness and rushed work, rather than through major problems of understanding. Make sure you take the time to plan and understand your assignments.

The assignment 'brief'

This may be longer than its name implies! The assignment brief includes all the instructions for an assignment and several other details, as you can see in the table below.

What will you find in a BTEC Level 3 National assignment brief?	
Content	**Details**
Title	This will link to the unit and learning outcomes
Format/style	Written assignment, presentation, demonstration etc
Preparation	Read case study, do research etc
Learning outcomes	These state the knowledge you must demonstrate to obtain a required grade
Grading criterion/ criteria covered	For example, P1, M1, D1
Individual/group work	Remember to identify your own contribution in any group work
Feedback	Tutor, peer review
Interim review dates	Dates to see your tutor
Final deadline	Last submission date

TOP TIP

Reading and understanding each assignment brief is vital. Ask your tutor if there's anything you don't understand.

Your centre's rules and regulations

Your centre will have several policies and guidelines about assignments, which you need to check carefully. Many, such as those listed below, relate to Edexcel policies and guidelines.

- The procedure to follow if you have a serious problem and can't meet a deadline. An extension may be granted.
- The penalty for missing a deadline without good reason.
- The penalty for copying someone else's work. This is usually severe, so never share your work (or CDs or USB flash drive) with anyone else, and don't borrow theirs.
- **Plagiarism** is also serious misconduct. This means copying someone's work or quoting from books and websites and pretending it is your own work.
- The procedure to follow if you disagree with the grade you are given.

Understanding the question or task

There are two aspects to a question or task. The first is the **command words**, which are described below. The second is the **presentation instructions**, which is what you are asked to do – don't write a report when you should be producing a chart!

Command words, such as 'explain', 'describe', 'analyse', 'evaluate' state how a question must be answered. You may be asked to 'describe' something at pass level, but you will need to do more, perhaps 'analyse' or 'evaluate', to achieve merit or distinction.

Many learners fail to achieve higher grades because they don't realise the difference between these words. Instead of analysing or evaluating they give an explanation instead. Adding more details won't achieve a higher grade – you need to change your whole approach to the answer.

The **grading grid** for each unit of your course gives you the command words, so that you know what to do to achieve a pass, merit or distinction. The tables that follow show you what is usually required when you see a particular command word. These are just examples to guide you, as the exact response will depend on the question. If you have any doubts, check with your tutor before you start work.

There are two important points to note.

- A command word such as 'create' or 'explain' may be repeated in the grading criteria for different grades. In these cases the complexity or range of the task itself increases at the higher grades.
- Command words vary depending on your vocational area. So Art and Design grading

grids may use different command words from Applied Science, for example.

TOP TIP

Look at this section again when you get your first assignment, and check the command words against these explanations.

To obtain a pass grade

To achieve a pass you must demonstrate that you understand the important facts relating to a topic and can state these clearly and concisely.

Command words for a pass	Meaning
Create (or produce)	Make, invent or construct an item.
Describe	Give a clear, straightforward description that includes all the main points and links these together logically.
Define	Clearly explain what a particular term means and give an example, if appropriate, to show what you mean.
Explain … how/why	Set out in detail the meaning of something, with reasons. It is often helpful to give an example of what you mean. Start with the topic then give the 'how' or 'why'.
Identify	Distinguish and state the main features or basic facts relating to a topic.
Interpret	Define or explain the meaning of something.
Illustrate	Give examples to show what you mean.
List	Provide the information required in a list rather than in continuous writing.
Outline	Write a clear description that includes all the main points but avoid going into too much detail.
Plan (or devise)	Work out and explain how you would carry out a task or activity.
Select (and present) information	Identify relevant information to support the argument you are making and communicate this in an appropriate way.
State	Write a clear and full account.
Undertake	Carry out a specific activity.
Examples:	
Identify the main features on a digital camera.	
Outline the steps to take to carry out research for an assignment.	

To obtain a merit grade

To obtain a merit you must prove that you can apply your knowledge in a specific way.

Command words for a merit	Meaning
Analyse	Identify separate factors and say how they relate to each other and how each one relates to the topic.
Classify	Sort your information into appropriate categories before presenting or explaining it.
Compare and contrast	Identify the main factors that apply in two or more situations and explain the similarities and differences or advantages and disadvantages.
Demonstrate	Provide several relevant examples or appropriate evidence which support the arguments you are making. In some vocational areas this may also mean giving a practical performance.
Discuss	Provide a thoughtful and logical argument to support the case you are making.
Explain (in detail)	Provide details and give reasons and/or evidence to clearly support the argument you are making.
Implement	Put into practice or operation. You may also have to interpret or justify the effect or result.
Interpret	Understand and explain an effect or result.
Justify	Give appropriate reasons to support your opinion or views and show how you arrived at these conclusions.
Relate/report	Give a full account, with reasons.
Research	Carry out a full investigation.
Specify	Provide full details and descriptions of selected items or activities.
Examples: Compare and contrast the performance of two different digital cameras. Explain in detail the steps to take to research an assignment.	

To obtain a distinction grade

To obtain a distinction you must prove that you can make a reasoned judgement based on appropriate evidence.

Command words for a distinction	Meaning
Analyse	Identify the key factors, show how they are linked, and explain the importance and relevance of each.
Assess	Give careful consideration to all the factors or events that apply, and identify which are the most important and relevant, with reasons.
Comprehensively explain	Give a very detailed explanation that covers all the relevant points, and give reasons for your views or actions.
Critically comment	Give your view after you have considered all the evidence, particularly the importance of both the relevant positive and negative aspects.
Evaluate	Review the information and then bring it together to form a conclusion. Give evidence to support each of your views or statements.
Evaluate critically	Review the information to decide the degree to which something is true, important or valuable. Then assess possible alternatives, taking into account their strengths and weaknesses if they were applied instead. Then give a precise and detailed account to explain your opinion.
Summarise	Identify/review the main relevant factors and/or arguments so that these are explained in a clear and concise manner.
Examples:	
Assess ten features commonly found on a digital camera.	
Analyse your own ability to carry out effective research for an assignment.	

TOP TIP

Check that you understand exactly how you need to demonstrate each of the learning outcomes specified in the assignment.

Responding positively

Assignments enable you to demonstrate what you know and how you can apply it. You should respond positively to the challenge and give it your best shot. Being well organised and having confidence in your own abilities helps too, and this is covered in the next section.

Key points

- Read instructions carefully so that you don't make mistakes that can easily be avoided, such as only doing part of the set task.
- Note the assignment deadline on your planner and any interim review dates. Schedule work around these dates to make the most of reviews with your tutor.
- Check your centre's policies relating to assignments, such as how to obtain an extension or query a final grade.
- Expect command words and/or the complexity of a task to be different at higher grades, because you have to demonstrate higher-level skills.

TOP TIP

All your assignments will relate to topics you have covered and work you have done in class. They're not meant to be a test to catch you out.

Action points

1 Check your ability to differentiate between different types of command words by doing this activity.

   a) Prepare a brief description of your usual lifestyle (pass level).

   b) Describe and justify your current lifestyle (merit level).

   c) Critically evaluate your current lifestyle (distinction level).

It would be a good idea to check that your answer is accurate and appropriate by showing it to your tutor at your next tutorial.

TOP TIP

When presenting evidence for an assessment, think about the person who will be looking through it. Plan your 'pitch' well and make it easy for the assessor to match your evidence against the grading criteria.

Sample assignment

All learners are different and will approach their assignments in different ways.
The sample assignment that follows shows how one learner answered a brief to achieve pass, merit and distinction level criteria. This learner work shows just one way in which these grading criteria can be evidenced. There are no standard or set answers. If you produce the required evidence for each task, then you will achieve the grading criteria covered by the assignment.

Front sheet

Make sure you complete the assignment front sheet details fully and correctly; the details let the assessor and the internal verifier know who the work belongs to.

Interim and final hand-in dates are provided to ensure that you can plan around exact deadlines and that all your work can be assessed within the same given timescales. Remember to check your centre's policy on meeting deadlines.

Remember to check the specific unit assessment criteria against the evidence you plan to submit. Written work (annotation) and spoken descriptions (presentation) support visual work and can both provide evidence for assessment.

Learner name		Assessor name
Daniel Tyson		Jackie Reid

Date issued	Completion date	Submitted on
10 September 2010	Interim: 16 November 2010 Final: 10 December 2010	10 December 2010

Qualification	Unit
BTEC Level 3 Diploma in Art and Design	Unit 1: Visual Recording in Art and Design

Assignment title	An exhibition on the human form

In this assessment you will have opportunities to provide evidence against the following criteria. Indicate the page numbers where the evidence can be found.

Criteria reference	To achieve the criteria the evidence must show that the learner is able to:	Task no.
P1	identify primary and secondary sources for recording	1, 2
P2	record visually	2, 3
P3	discuss visual recording in others' work	1, 2, 3
P4	review own visual recording	2, 3, 4, 5
P5	develop visual recording to produce effective outcomes	4, 5, 6
M1	research and respond to independently selected sources, consistently showing effective visual recording skills	2, 4, 6

This table identifies the unit grading criteria (which is mapped against assigned tasks in the brief) and indicates where you can find more details about the evidence required for assessment.

Signing (and dating) the document affirms that the work is authentic, belongs to you, does not breach copyright and is appropriate for assessment.

M2	show an individual approach to communicating, comparing, illustrating and expanding information and presenting work in a coherent and appropriate creative format	1, 2, 3, 4, 5, 6
D1	demonstrate independence, innovation and individuality in evaluating and using sources, integrating visual recording skills and in-depth understanding in communicating information	1, 2, 3, 4, 5, 6

Learner declaration

I certify that the work submitted for this assignment is my own and research sources are fully acknowledged.

Learner signature: *Daniel Tyson*   Date: *10 December 2010*

Assignment brief

The scenario will help you relate the assignment tasks to the real world of art and design.

The 'overview' acts as an introduction to the assignment and as a reference point for initial ideas. The 'evidence' directives prompt ideas development and influence work in progress.

Unit title	Unit 1: Visual Recording in Art and Design
Qualification	BTEC Level 3 Diploma in Art and Design
Start date	10 September 2010
Interim deadline	16 November 2010
Deadline date	10 December 2010
Assessor	Jackie Reid

Assignment title	An exhibition of the human form

The purpose of this assignment is to:
develop and extend your visual language skills and understanding by working from life models.

Scenario
The local art gallery and museum is mounting an exhibition of artwork based on the human form. The exhibition curators have asked for a submission of work to form part of the display. At an interim stage in the project (16 November 2010), you will present your ongoing work to your peers, tutors and gallery curators. This will determine which pieces are selected for the exhibition.

Overview and evidence
For this assignment you need to prepare a series of life studies. From these you should develop 2D finished pieces for the exhibition. You will need to prepare an interim presentation of your plans on 16 November 2010, showing your ideas and preliminary work for your final pieces. This presentation can be designed and presented in any way you feel is appropriate for the audience, including digitally. You will present to the gallery curators and a panel of tutors who will then make their selection of pieces for the exhibition. Your final artwork will be submitted on 10 December 2010. Please also include an ongoing report/journal to record your work for each task of this assignment.

Task 1 – Discussing the work of others
There will be a series of study sessions held throughout this assignment on approaches to the human form. These will include short lectures and discussions looking at the work of other artists. In these sessions you will be working individually and in small groups. You will be able to discuss the approaches and techniques the artists have used to record visual information (P3) and take notes, make rough sketches and record your observations during each study session. Think about how the artists have used and selected sources for their work, and include your findings in the notes you keep. You can apply the understanding gained from this task to help you identify sources for your own work (P1) as you think about the pieces you would like to produce for the exhibition. Record your ideas in your assignment journal.

This provides evidence towards P1 and P3

To build on your evidence for the pass criteria, you will need to show that you can work independently to explore and compare the work of others in this field. To do this you will need to research some of the artists you have looked at in the lectures and discussions, to find out more about them and how they work. Alternatively, you can research some other artists who use the human form in their work. You can show that you are expanding your understanding by recording your thoughts and ideas and by showing examples of your research. Aim to reach conclusions about the work by other artists that you have looked at, and think about how this may help you to develop your own working practice.

This provides evidence towards M2

To build on your M2 evidence to meet D1, you will need to use your analysis of other artist's work and demonstrate in your own notes and sketches that you have your own ideas and individual approach when it comes to using resources, integrating visual recording skills and communicating information.

This provides evidence towards D1

'Introducer' study sessions provide opportunities to work with your peers, which can generate ideas and discussions and build your confidence to sketch out your own ideas and investigate the work of others.

It is important that your research into other artists is in context. Informed secondary research, working to a clear investigative plan, can underpin your primary research and ideas development. Avoid unstructured research, which might cloud your analysis and evaluation.

Task 2 provides a list of specific actions, in the visual recording of the figure, to be completed in order to meet the unit pass criteria at stage 1 (P1, P2 and P4).

Additional briefing guidance is provided here to meet M1 and D1 grading criteria. This is really useful in improving attainment and making progress through the unit, and you should read it carefully.

Task 2 – Visual recording: the figure
You will be working from life models. You will start by working from short poses, and go on to longer poses.

- Try to draw quickly, using a faint line to begin with.
- Draw the whole figure, not part of it – don't worry if it takes a while to be able to do this, you will find that you will speed up as you go along.
- Draw from the middle out (this will have been dicussed in lectures) – and avoid doing an outline only.
- Start thinking about the suitability of different media for certain tasks, such as expressing volume with tonal media.

Stage 1
Explore the human form, observing different aspects of structure, form and movement (P1). Record a range of different poses, using the formal elements of line, tone, shape and surface (P2). Explore informal methods of recording that express ideas and feelings in a variety of quick studies using experimental mark-making. Use analytical methods to explore accurate recording of the human structure in different poses: use appropriate measuring methods, focusing on proportion, perspective, space-shape relationships, and angles and curves (P4).

This provides evidence towards P1, P2 and P4

You can increase your grade by demonstrating an independent approach. You can record from the figure using your own ideas about how to work with different media. Think about how you can apply media and visual language to record defined aspects of the figure, through form, volume, movement, contrast and so on. You can practise your skills by working on your own drawings outside of the sessions. You can make your recording effective by looking carefully at the subject and recording what you see and feel. Reflect on the work you have produced and decide what to do next. Artists often return to their subject to get more information or to adapt their ideas. Make notes to record your thinking, and show how you are going to refine your work.

This provides evidence towards M1

You can extend your grade by independently reaching conclusions about your working practices. You should show how you have understood the work of others and used this to inform your approach to recording. You will need to show innovative approaches to recording from the subject, by exploring, combining and consolidating your understanding and skills in using media and visual language.

This provides evidence towards D1

Stage 2
Using your investigations into the work of other artists (from Task 1), demonstrate how your own work is influenced or inspired by selected images of others' work (P3, P4). As you work through Stage 1 of this task, build on and develop your research into appropriate contexts (P1). Investigate and explore appropriate 2D mark-making and techniques for recording from the model, such as charcoal, graphite, chalks, brush and ink, paint, canvas, board and papers (P2). Explore the potential of selected tools and techniques in recording to communicate different moods, such as strong lighting to evoke contrast and depth or mixed media to communicate qualities of the structure of the body and the surface of skin. Review your progress, critically analysing the development of your studies (P4).

This provides evidence towards P1, P2, P3 and P4

Stage 2 summarises the evidence that should have been produced for Task 1. You can see that it's important to read the whole assignment brief before starting work to avoid missing essential guidance and information.

Task 3 relates to ideas development leading to the final presentation of 2D work, and a useful checklist is provided to underpin the evidence required to meet the grading criteria.

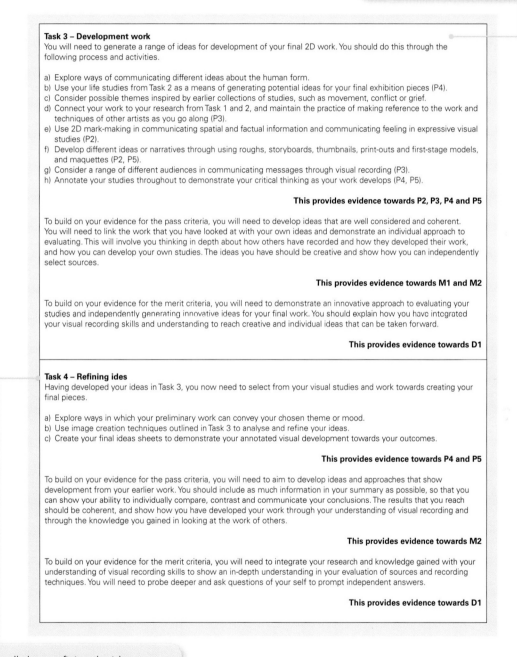

Task 3 – Development work

You will need to generate a range of ideas for development of your final 2D work. You should do this through the following process and activities.

a) Explore ways of communicating different ideas about the human form.
b) Use your life studies from Task 2 as a means of generating potential ideas for your final exhibition pieces (P4).
c) Consider possible themes inspired by earlier collections of studies, such as movement, conflict or grief.
d) Connect your work to your research from Task 1 and 2, and maintain the practice of making reference to the work and techniques of other artists as you go along (P3).
e) Use 2D mark-making in communicating spatial and factual information and communicating feeling in expressive visual studies (P2).
f) Develop different ideas or narratives through using roughs, storyboards, thumbnails, print-outs and first-stage models, and maquettes (P2, P5).
g) Consider a range of different audiences in communicating messages through visual recording (P3).
h) Annotate your studies throughout to demonstrate your critical thinking as your work develops (P4, P5).

This provides evidence towards P2, P3, P4 and P5

To build on your evidence for the pass criteria, you will need to develop ideas that are well considered and coherent. You will need to link the work that you have looked at with your own ideas and demonstrate an individual approach to evaluating. This will involve you thinking in depth about how others have recorded and how they developed their work, and how you can develop your own studies. The ideas you have should be creative and show how you can independently select sources.

This provides evidence towards M1 and M2

To build on your evidence for the merit criteria, you will need to demonstrate an innovative approach to evaluating your studies and independently generating innovative ideas for your final work. You should explain how you have integrated your visual recording skills and understanding to reach creative and individual ideas that can be taken forward.

This provides evidence towards D1

Task 4 – Refining ides

Having developed your ideas in Task 3, you now need to select from your visual studies and work towards creating your final pieces.

a) Explore ways in which your preliminary work can convey your chosen theme or mood.
b) Use image creation techniques outlined in Task 3 to analyse and refine your ideas.
c) Create your final ideas sheets to demonstrate your annotated visual development towards your outcomes.

This provides evidence towards P4 and P5

To build on your evidence for the pass criteria, you will need to aim to develop ideas and approaches that show development from your earlier work. You should include as much information in your summary as possible, so that you can show your ability to individually compare, contrast and communicate your conclusions. The results that you reach should be coherent, and show how you have developed your work through your understanding of visual recording and through the knowledge you gained in looking at the work of others.

This provides evidence towards M2

To build on your evidence for the merit criteria, you will need to integrate your research and knowledge gained with your understanding of visual recording skills to show an in-depth understanding in your evaluation of sources and recording techniques. You will need to probe deeper and ask questions of your self to prompt independent answers.

This provides evidence towards D1

Task 4 is all about refining the ideas development initiated through Task 3 and involves analysis of your own work (leading to coherent comparisons and evaluation of your own and others' work).

Task 5 is the culmination of all the evidence-gathering, and concerns the presentation of final ideas. This provides an opportunity to improve on and extend earlier work and move towards the final piece.

Task 5 – Presenting your final ideas

You must now prepare a presentation for the exhibition curators to show your final ideas and preliminary work for your artwork pieces on the human form. The date for the presentation is 16 November.

a) Research different presentation methods, given your target audience of gallery curators.
b) Explore and experiment with appropriate presentation methods. You can use digital presentation techniques – including video, slide, PowerPoint and audiovisual displays – or deliver a verbal presentation or a demonstration, or produce a display, or use a combination of any of these methods.
c) Select appropriate information and images from your studies for your presentation.
d) Select an appropriate presentation method and develop your presentation.
e) Give a mock presentation to peer group and tutors before the final one to the gallery curators.

This provides evidence towards P4 and P5

To build on your evidence for the pass criteria, you will need to show how you have compared your work, used the information gained from looking at the work of others, and developed your understanding of visual recording as you progressed through the assignment. You need to evidence this – use notes, refer to visual examples, look to illustrate the points you make clearly and coherently. If you say you have learnt something, or changed your ideas because of your evaluation, refer to exact visual examples to make your point.

This provides evidence towards M2

To build on your evidence for the merit criteria, you will need to extend your work further by showing how you have independently integrated your understanding of visual recording and how it is used to communicate ideas. You should refer to others' work, explain the ideas and concepts you learnt through evaluating their work, and show how you applied this understanding to developing your own work in an individual and innovative way.

This provides evidence towards D1

Task 6

Using the information and feedback from your presentation to the curators, and feedback from your tutor and peers, select and develop a final painting to be hung in the exhibition. You should bring together your understanding of visual recording, and the ideas shown in your developmental work that the curators singled out as being suitable for the exhibition.

All paintings should be produced to a professional standard, on properly prepared grounds, as this work will be seen in a public exhibition.

This provides further evidence towards P5

To build on your evidence for pass criteria you will need to:

Use your studies to develop an individual approach to producing the work. You might achieve this through using materials, visual language and visual recording in an imaginative and creative format. You should show a consistent approach to independently using in-depth recording skills.

This provides further evidence towards M1 and M2

To build on your evidence for merit criteria you will need to:

Extend your work by integrating your visual recording skills and producing work that shows an innovative approach to realising creative intentions.

This provides further evidence towards D1

Task 6 allows for personal evaluation, analysis and reflection on your own (and others') work, leading to a clearer understanding of visual recording in art and design.

> You can use this list of resources to help develop your ideas for the assignment.

Sources of information

Beverly H R – *Drawing Lessons from the Great Masters* (Watson-Guptill, 1989) ISBN 9780823014019
Ching F D K – *Design Drawing* (John Wiley & Sons Inc, 1997) ISBN 9780471286547
Ching F D K – *Drawing: a Creative Process* (John Wiley & Sons Inc, 1989) ISBN 9780471289685
Hazel H – *The Encyclopedia of Drawing Techniques* (Search Press, 2004) ISBN 9781844480197
Metzger R – *Gustav Klimt – Drawings and Watercolours* (Thames & Hudson, 2005) ISBN 9780500238264
Muybridge E – *The Human Figure in Motion* (Dover, 2000) ISBN 9780486202044
Picasso P ed Glimcher A B – *Je Suis Le Cahier – Sketchbooks of Picasso* (Thames & Hudson, 1996) ISBN 9780500279229
Peterson B – *Learning to See Creatively* (Amphoto Books, revised edition, 2003) ISBN 9780817441814
Scarfe G – *Drawing Blood* (Little, Brown, 2005) ISBN 9780316729529
Simpson I – *Drawing, Seeing and Observation* (A&C Black, 2003) ISBN 9780713668780
Treib M – *Drawing/Thinking* (Routledge, 2008) ISBN 9780415775618

This brief has been verified as being fit for purpose			
Assessor	Ms J Read		
Signature	Jackie Read	Date	8 September 2010
Internal verifier	Ms K Armani		
Signature	Kay Armani	Date	8 September 2010

Sample learner work

Galleries are a great place for looking at others' work with a view to influencing your own.

Investigation of other artists' work influences primary and secondary resources and is essential to research.

Sample learner work: page 1

An exhibition of the human form

Task 1

I have never really tackled drawing people so when we were given our assignment sheets to go through, I was a bit worried that I might not be able to get very far with it – or I might get bored with all that life drawing. I liked the idea of taking the human figure into our own ideas for final work and I've already had some ideas for this part of the assignment.

We visited the gallery to meet the curators and view the space we were going to have for our work. We had a brief preview of some of the artists' 2D and 3D figure work. There was also a video by a contemporary artist who had explored the idea of the rituals humans perform in their everyday lives. I was able to make some sketches and notes but we weren't allowed to take photos. The idea of exhibiting my own figure work here is scary after seeing the artists' skilful work and brilliant ideas. (P1, P2)

Looking at the work of different artists in the slide show sessions showed me lots of ways to make figure studies. Some of the images were incredibly skilful, especially the 3D figures – Rodin's sculptures of *The Burghers of Calais* really impressed me – it's bigger than life-size and has incredible detail in the hands and features of the group who are tied together with rope. But what was great about it were the expressions and feelings of despair, anger and tension in their faces and in the gestures of their hands. The way that Rodin had carved their heads with some looking upwards and some down and to the side also gave the feeling of dignity and a sense of endurance of suffering. By joining the figures together with rope and making each have a different but connected pose, Rodin created a sense of the whole sculpture working as one piece. But I also felt that there was a feeling of isolation and helplessness in the closed and inward mood of each figure. I've found out that there's a copy of this sculpture in the gardens by the Houses of Parliament, which the public can go into – so I'm definitely off to see that! (P3, D1)

We also looked at some figure paintings and sculptures from early 20th century art of Cubism and Futurism. I liked the way the artists had broken up the figures into fragments which gave the figures a sense of energy and in the way they had used the paint to create movement. These reminded me of camera shots of sports figures and then I discovered that an artist called Muybridge had already done some early photographic experiments to explore movement in figures, which might have influenced these artists. We looked at straight portrait artists too, from 17th to the 20th century, but I found these less interesting as I feel drawn to artists who use figures to portray a situation or a mood – though I found the use of very strong shadows in Rembrandt's portraits gave the figure a strong presence and 3D quality. We looked at some images from more recent times – these include Lucien Freud, Henry Moore and David Hockney. These people had all worked from the figure and taken their ideas into different formats. I thought Hockney's splash paintings were really good – simple compositions, strong colours and a kind of still photographic quality. We also looked at Jenny Saville's work, which again I really liked – the idea of using scale and viewpoint as key compositional devices really impressed me. The figure work we looked at was clearly related to the task we were going to do – work from the figure. I was also interested in the idea that some of the artists had developed ideas and figure work beyond purely the seen image – some of it was kind of felt. There was a Matisse picture called *The Dance* which I also really liked. (P3, M2)

During our seminar group sessions we had a visiting practitioner who showed us his portfolio of life studies, paintings and photographs of his sculptural pieces. We also had the opportunity to present our notes and studies to him, and we shared some great discussions about his work and the artists' work we've looked at. Now I'm much more interested in the next part of the project – which is lots of life drawing. (P3, D1)

Sharing ideas and discussing your own and others' work is an excellent way to improve personal and professional skills.

Developing your ideas through media manipulation provides a basis for analysis and reflection, and can improve your grade.

Mapping activities against unit assessment criteria is a good way to monitor your progress and improve your attainment levels. Critical evaluation and reflection are integral to progress.

Sample learner work: page 2

Task 2

For this task I've produced loads of 2D studies in different media – some really awful ones too, where I've got the figure out of proportion or made a complete hash of the feet and hands. These parts are really difficult, and the head too. it seems to make such a difference to the figure if the head, feet and hands are in proportion and connect to the body. I liked the way the tutor called the feet the roots of the body, the hands the direction for the branches of the body and the head describes what type of tree it is – the model's character. To practise drawing heads, hands and feet, I've looked at Durer's drawings of hands and also copied some of the drawings from a book on the Old Masters. I've used myself and friends too as models for developing my skills. (P1, P2)

The more successful studies so far are the very quick charcoal studies where I have had to respond immediately to the model and not think about the detail. At the beginning I thought these were the worst, but when I laid them out for an assessment session, I could see they had the most sense of movement and I had caught the character of the pose with a few strong lines and quickly sketched in tones.

Last week we were introduced to some more drawing techniques, and ways of combining materials. I found this quite interesting, as I hadn't thought about working with wet and dry materials on the same piece of work. I had always assumed that life drawing meant focusing on the figure – which it does – but I hadn't connected with the idea that you could explore visual language and media in life drawing at the same time. This made the whole process much more creative, rather than being purely academic – my tutor said the phrase 'it won't be as dry' – I think I know what she meant. (M1)

I visited London at the weekend and managed to get to see Rodin's *Burghers of Calais* at Westminster. It was even more exciting than I had imagined from the slides and images on the internet. I did loads of sketches from different angles and began to understand how a sculpture changes as you move round it and offers you different forms and shapes each time you move. I wished I'd borrowed a video camera from college, but I did manage to take lots of shots and make a brief video with my mobile phone. (M2, D1)

My tutor has suggested I spend some time working on developing my 2D work towards possible ideas for an outcome. Yesterday I tried painting the figure and ended up with mostly muddy colours and an almost completely obliterated figure underneath. My tutor gave us a brilliant demonstration and advised us to use a limited colour palette, so tomorrow I'll give it another go. (D1)

I had a tutorial aimed at evaluating my work so far (P4). My tutor said positive things about my work and the progress I had made, and has definitely given me motivation to persist. She offered me some really useful ways I could develop my work towards a 2D theme. She suggested I find some of my own primary sources for figures in movement and I came up with the idea of sketching my family to help me with gaining skills. I like the idea of doing a kind of seated figure for the final piece, but exploring colour – I have enjoyed the painting part, once I got over the muddy colours – I looked again at Hockney and Matisse, and I have decided that my interest really lies with working a design into the final piece, but still making it a piece of work painted from life. I really like the idea of two things going together – juxtaposition or duality – so a colour design is also a life painting – this is the kind of thing you see when you look at Rembrandt or Freud close up, or in details in books – the materials both record and also have a language of their own. I looked at some work by an artist called Poussin, and made a couple of studies from a piece called *The Triumph of Pan*. (P3)

Task 3

I'm now seriously into the idea of a final life-based 2D piece. I still need to practise painting, but have found that using colour very thinly – combining watercolours with acrylics and working over these colours with washes – creates interesting and effective areas on the canvas. (P2, P5)

Listening to feedback and reviewing others' work can enrich your own outcomes through the reflective process.

Experimenting with new techniques and working processes, implementing individual study skills and reflecting on your own and others' work will assist your progress.

Working within specific timelines is a crucial part of getting your assignment completed, and is an important skill to master.

I've discovered an inspiring Canadian artist called Betty Goodwin. She has done some large-scale drawings of what looks like figures under the water. What I like about them is they are almost abstract and often reduced to blurred amorphous shapes almost like eels or fish. But I also want to keep looking at them as they feel quite mysterious, even sad, as if the figure is drowning or has drowned and is half suspended in the water. So I'm inspired to try out her approach with the sketches I've done so far. (P3)

I'm definitely decided on continuing the life model for my final piece. I think there is a strong tradition of working from life, yet producing abstract or painterly pieces – I really like this approach – it's not what I expected at all from life drawing! (P4, M1, M2, D1)

Task 4

This is it. The deadline for completion of the studies before presenting to the group is coming up and I feel I need to do much more to my work. I've put together a short PowerPoint presentation to show the development of my ideas for the final piece – I did explore some ideas about a kind of classical painting with two figures, but I don't think I have the skills in understanding the figure to be able to construct a convincing and effective final piece. I have produced lots of drawings, looked at some examples of artists' work and explored composition and materials. I intend to combine my understanding of recording and looking with the interest I have with using media. (P4, P5)

I've created my final ideas sheets. I have included some compositional drawings. Now I've got to select from all the rough studies to make a presentation to the group and to the gallery curators. The main thing I've got to consider is how to get across how I got from the first task of looking at artists' studies of the human form to my final ideas for the painting, and why I have decided to approach the theme the way I have. (M2, D1)

Task 5

After going through all the options for presenting, I've decided on which images I am going to use in the PowerPoint presentation. We have to do a trial run in front of our group, before we do the big presentation to the curators. A friend who's doing the media course is going to make a video of me presenting my display and talking to my group. Then I'm going to use the video to support my big presentation to the gallery and tutors. I'll be OK talking to my friends, but I'm feeling very shaky about talking to the experts. (P5)

I've worked out what I need to do to display the work to the best advantage. I've talked to the caretaker and tutors to get hold of display boards and I've selected an area in the drawing studio where there's good lighting and enough space to give the presentation and for Rob to make the video. Rob and me have done a trial run-through and I can see where I need to fill the gaps and prevent awkward pauses. I've designed my crib sheet and also given one to Rob so he knows which bits are coming next and what images to focus on as I'm talking. (M2)

I did some research into what makes an effective presentation and managed to find several examples on the internet – also one which included a video as well as a display and discussion. These were really helpful and helped me to design my crib sheet and consider the order I need to put the points I want to get across. I think the video will help to provide interest, as I'll be using it as a different method of communicating my ideas. I like the idea of involving the audience and inviting them to ask questions as I think this will make me less nervous than silence! (D1) I'm really pleased that I can use the PowerPoint slides and short snippets from the video in the final presentation to the curators.

I've now completed all the tasks for this assignment and got great feedback from the presentation, which has really boosted my confidence. I was very pleased to get a distinction for this assignment and now feel really prepared for more complicated design projects next term.

Describing formal elements in a presentation can be done through annotation, visually (through the use of mixed media) and verbally. Task 5 brings the whole process to a conclusion with the presentation of the work.

Presenting your own work in a professional context is demanding. However, it provides an opportunity to collate and confirm research, ideas development and proposals.

Using PowerPoint software is useful for presenting work in a methodical way (P3).

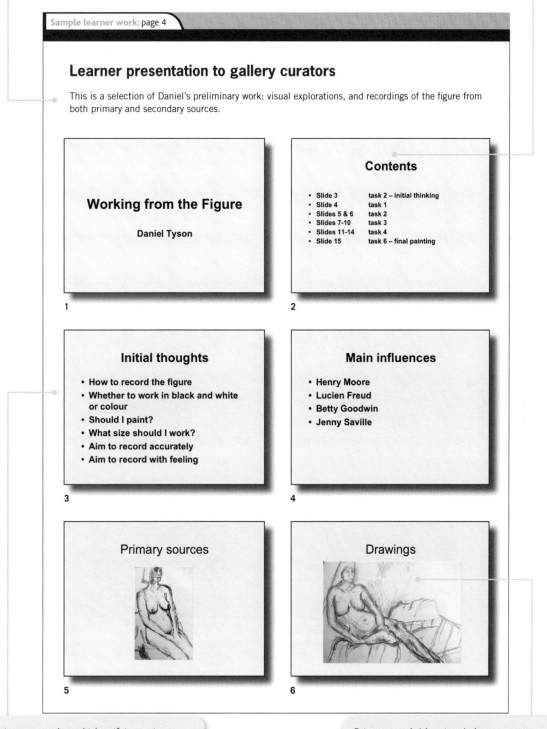

Sample learner work: page 4

Learner presentation to gallery curators

This is a selection of Daniel's preliminary work: visual explorations, and recordings of the figure from both primary and secondary sources.

Working from the Figure

Daniel Tyson

1

Contents

- Slide 3   task 2 – initial thinking
- Slide 4   task 1
- Slides 5 & 6   task 2
- Slides 7-10   task 3
- Slides 11-14   task 4
- Slide 15   task 6 – final painting

2

Initial thoughts

- How to record the figure
- Whether to work in black and white or colour
- Should I paint?
- What size should I work?
- Aim to record accurately
- Aim to record with feeling

3

Main influences

- Henry Moore
- Lucien Freud
- Betty Goodwin
- Jenny Saville

4

Primary sources

5

Drawings

6

Charting research and identifying primary and secondary resources and influences provides evidence to meet P1.

Primary work (drawings) demonstrates exploratory and appropriate mark-making skills underpinning P2 and P3 criteria.

Working on primary and secondary research (slides 7–9) the evidence combines with earlier investigations to provide a broad range of evidence to meet M1.

By using diverse and experimental recording skills, the range of 2D primary evidence is considered to meet the M2 grading criteria.

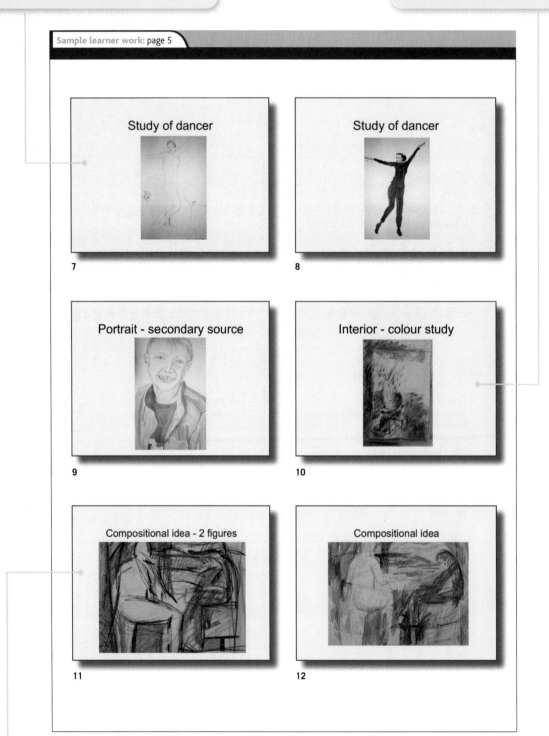

Sample learner work: page 5

Study of dancer

7

Study of dancer

8

Portrait - secondary source

9

Interior - colour study

10

Compositional idea - 2 figures

11

Compositional idea

12

Experimenting with techniques and processes to communicate visual 2D information evidences individuality and confirms a broad range of skills to meet M1 and M2 grading criteria.

Evidence of refinement of ideas, through careful and informed analysis, allows for individuality in presenting effective outcomes (M1).

Experimental work (slides 1–14) demonstrates independence and innovation in selective primary research, ideas development and presentation (D1).

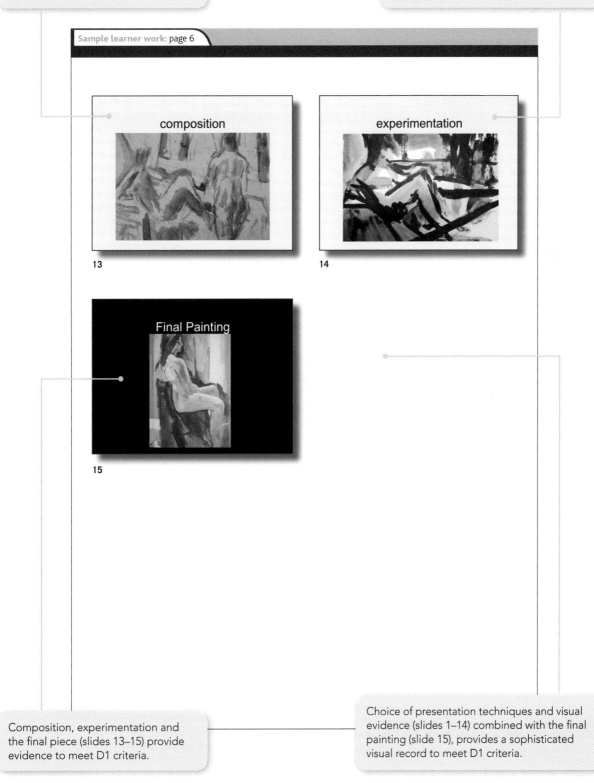

Sample learner work: page 6

composition

13

experimentation

14

Final Painting

15

Composition, experimentation and the final piece (slides 13–15) provide evidence to meet D1 criteria.

Choice of presentation techniques and visual evidence (slides 1–14) combined with the final painting (slide 15), provides a sophisticated visual record to meet D1 criteria.

Observation record

Observation records (or witness statements) give you important feedback and provide evidence that you have completed practical work.

The observation record must include a description of the activity undertaken, as it may only relate to part of the assessment evidence (for a particular task or tasks).

Learner name	Daniel Tyson
Qualification	BTEC Level 3 Diploma in Art and Design
Unit number and title	Unit 1: Visual Recording in Art and Design

Description of activity undertaken (please be as specific as possible)

Presentation to gallery curators, tutors and peers.

Assessment and grading criteria

Partial coverage of P3, P4 and M2.

How the activity meets the requirements of the assessment and grading criteria

Daniel gave a really good presentation. He discussed his own visual recording and the approaches he adopted (P4). He was able to relate this to the work he had looked at, and demonstrated a consistent ability to expand the information to show coherent views (P3). He had clearly gained a lot of understanding from looking at the work of others and was able to relate that directly to the ways he developed his own recording techniques. As he developed his ideas about the figure, he produced work that showed a number of potential routes, and his presentation demonstrated an ability to compare information. The PowerPoint presentation was well supported by handouts, and the use of a video camera to record the presentation was a well-thought-out idea. His presentation and discussion showed he could adopt an individual approach to presenting his work in a creative manner (M2), and he showed independence and innovation in the way he developed his presentation skills. He demonstrated an in-depth understanding of the potential in figure-based work, and communicated this in the language he used.

Learner signature	Daniel Tyson	Date	14 January 2011
Assessor signature	Jackie Read	Date	16 November 2010
Assessor name	Ms J Read		

Your tutor will give clear feedback which should also tell you what you need to do to improve your work.

Observation records must be signed and dated by the learner and assessor to be a valid part of the assessment documentation and process.

Assessor's comments

You should take the opportunity to provide feedback on the assignment; for example, set out what you enjoyed and what you found challenging. This is a good way of improving your work by thinking about how you did.

'Y' and 'N' mean 'Yes' and 'No'. This shows whether or not the evidence produced meets the grading criteria.

Qualification	BTEC Level 3 Diploma in Art and Design	Year	2010–2011
Unit number and title	Unit 1: Visual Recording in Art and Design	Learner name	Daniel Tyson

Grading criteria	Achieved?
P1 identify primary and secondary sources for recording	Y
P2 record visually	Y
P3 discuss visual recording in others' work	Y
P4 review own visual recording	Y
P5 develop visual recording to produce effective outcomes	Y
M1 research and respond to independently selected sources, consistently showing effective visual recording skills	Y
M2 show an individual approach to communicating, comparing, illustrating and expanding information and presenting work in a coherent and appropriate creative format	Y
D1 demonstrate independence, innovation and individuality in evaluating and using sources, integrating visual recording skills and in-depth understanding in communicating information	Y

Learner feedback

I found this assignment very time-consuming but I learned so much about the human structure, especially proportion and perspective – it has really improved my tonal drawing and I was pleased with the effect using mixed media and colour to make the work really interesting – I found the colour had its own language and it would almost say 'I'm made of paint' to the viewer. If I allowed the paint to run and almost stain the canvas it got really interesting. I really enjoyed the duality of allowing materials to have their own language whilst still recording from the figure. I found the presentation to the gallery really challenging and I was very nervous. Using a video I had made previously of a presentation I did of my work to my seminar group really helped me to gain more confidence and I enjoyed answering questions and discussing my work with the gallery curators. However, I don't think this part of the assignment was my strong point.

Assessor feedback

Daniel, I'm really pleased with the mature way you tackled this lengthy project and worked hard to meet all the deadlines too. You have shown development in your drawing skills, particularly in your experimental use of drawing and painting materials. You have sourced your life studies and visited different galleries, to expand the work taken place in the studio. Your series of watercolour and acrylic studies are good, and the gallery curators have asked that our graphic design group of learners might be able to use these in their designs for the promotional material for the exhibition! Well done indeed.

You have written an extensive and articulate ongoing journal of your progress throughout the assignment and it is clear that you have a mature understanding of your ability but you need to develop your practical skills. I am impressed with the way you researched different artists and independently discovered the art of Betty Goodwin. It was interesting to see the ways in which you connected with her work in your use of materials and media. Your first-hand studies from the figure show developing recording skills with depiction of scale, form and proportion.

You put together an articulate and very well-informed digital presentation for your group and tutors, together with the gallery curators. The feedback from the gallery was very positive. They were impressed with your ability to communicate, illustrate and expand your ideas in such depth and also to hold their interest throughout.

You have covered the set tasks and achieved partial coverage of the criteria for this unit. What you have learned from this project will give you an advantage in your assignments for the units to come.

You should always pay attention to the assessor feedback. It will help you to understand what has been achieved and what still needs to be achieved.

An action plan is a very useful tool. It shows you what you need to do to improve further work, and helps you develop your skills.

Action plan

For future development, you should concentrate more on your studio work rather than your research. You will also need to link your own work to your research.

You reflected in your journal that you need to concentrate more on developing your studio and technical skills, and you would definitely benefit from engaging more in technical activities when using your research materials.

You could look in more detail at the various characteristics of artists' work in relation to specific media and particular intentions. For example:
- why do some artists explore our relationship with illusion and make us question the nature of the painting versus the photograph (see, for example the work of Chuck Close)
- why do some other artists force us to always recognise the energy and personality of the maker through using expressive marks?

These and other questions can form the basis of interesting, productive visual and contextual investigations that can produce personally involved work. Keep up the good work and maintain your high level of motivation and independence.

Assessor signature	Jackie Reid	Date	17 January 2011
Learner signature	Daniel Tyson	Date	19 January 2011

Step Seven: Work productively as a member of a group

Case study: Teams

Lauren, Hussein, Magda and Awais have formed a group to work on a live project. The brief is to design an indoor soft-play area for Key Stage 1 students in a local primary school. The brief requires the learners to produce ideas and develop designs. They need to produce draft layouts, technical drawings for presentations, and scale models.

Each project group has been given a set of basic key contexts and ideas for working successfully as a team and asked to work through this material and address any questions it raises.

Before starting the assignment, the group decides to look at how they would work best together. They decide that a team needs:

- complementary skills
- common purpose and performance goals
- a common approach
- mutual accountability
- personal, learning and thinking skills such as effective participators, team workers, independent enquirers, creative thinkers, self-managers and reflective learners.

They decide that to be successful they must:

- study the brief
- assign responsibilities to each team member
- put together a timeline for the project
- ensure that they meet all the requirements in the brief, and try to develop them further.

The group also thinks about what roles individual members would need to take on, and whether they would need to take on multiple roles. Along with a team leader, they decide that they would need people responsible for:

- coming up with ideas
- thinking about how the best idea would actually be implemented
- presenting the ideas
- producing technical drawings
- producing scale models, including sourcing any necessary materials.

Lauren's group decide that the time spent on thinking about how best a team works should put them in a good position for the rest of the project.

Reflection points

When working in a team do you go straight into the assignment or do you think about the team and its members' strengths and weaknesses beforehand?

Do you think that working groups have any generic characteristics?

What are the essential characteristics of a good team?

What do you think makes a good team leader or project manager?

In your private life, you can choose your own friends, whereas at work you are paid to work alongside many people, whether you like them or not. This applies at school or college too. Hopefully, by now, you've outgrown wanting to only work with your best friends on every project.

You may not be keen on everyone in your team, but you should still be pleasant and co-operative. This may be harder if you are working with a partner than in a large group.

Sometimes you may be the group leader. This may inspire you, or fill you with dread. You won't be expected to develop team-leader skills overnight, but it helps if you know the basics.

First, you should understand how groups and teams work and why good teamwork is considered vital by employers.

Working in groups and teams

If you have a full-time or part-time job, you already belong to a working group, or team. At school or college your class is an example of a working group.

All working groups have some common characteristics:

- doing the same type of work – though in the workplace you probably have different roles or responsibilities
- a group leader or supervisor
- a reason for working together, such as studying for the same qualification or tackling an area of work too large for someone to do alone
- group members are dependent on each other in some way; at work you may have to cover someone's workload if they are absent
- group members concentrate on their individual achievements and success.

A team is different. As a team member you have a specific objective to achieve **together** – and this is more important than the goals of individual team members.

TOP TIP

Understanding how groups and teams function will help you be a better team worker and a better team leader.

These are the characteristics of a team.

- Team members have a team goal which is more important than any personal goals.
- Team members have complementary skills so that the team can achieve more than individuals working alone could achieve.
- Work is allocated to play to each person's strengths and talents.
- The team members give each other encouragement and support.
- There is collective responsibility for achieving the goal.

A good team leader acts as facilitator and motivator, and gives practical support and guidance.

Working in a team has many benefits. Team members can learn from each other and combine their skills to do a better job more quickly. Working with other people is often more enjoyable than working alone, too. Many industries rely heavily on efficient group working, from IT teams to health workers and the emergency services.

TOP TIP

Focusing on the task rather than on personalities is the first step in learning to work with different people whose views may not match your own.

There are many benefits to be gained from working as a team.

Being a good team member

Everyone wants team members who are talented, positive, cheerful and full of energy. These are the key areas to focus on if you wish to be a good team member.

- **Your social skills.** This includes being courteous, treating other people as you wish to be treated, saying 'please' when you want something, and thanking people who do you a favour.

- **Your temperament**. Expect people to have different views and opinions from you, and don't take offence if someone disagrees with you. If you lose your temper easily, learn to walk away before you say something you may regret.

- **Your communication skills.** This includes talking and listening!

Practise saying what you mean clearly, accurately and succinctly. Be prepared to give good reasons to justify your arguments and ideas.

Allow people to finish what they're saying, without interruption, before you talk. Never shout people down. Think before you speak so that you don't upset people with tactless remarks. If you inadvertently do so, apologise.

- **Your commitment.** Always keep your promises and never let anyone down when they are depending upon you. Always do your fair share of the work, even if you don't agree with all the decisions made by your team. Tell people promptly if you are having problems, so there is time to solve them. Be loyal to your team when you're talking to other people.

Being the team leader

It can be difficult to strike a balance between leading the team and working with friends. You need to inspire and motivate your team without being bossy or critical.

Important points to remember about being a team leader

- Lead by example. Stay pleasant, consistent and control your temper, even under pressure.
- Everyone is different. Your ways of working may not always be the best.
- Be prepared to listen and contribute positively to a discussion.
- Encourage quieter team members to join in discussions by asking for their views.
- Be prepared to do whatever you ask other people to do.
- Note down what you say you will do, so that you don't forget.
- Discuss alternatives with people rather than giving orders.
- Be sensitive to other people's feelings. They may have personal problems or issues that affect their behaviour.
- Learn the art of persuasion.
- Act as peacemaker. Help people reach a compromise when necessary.
- Give team members the credit for their hard work or good ideas.
- Admit your mistakes. Look for a positive solution and think about what can be learned for the future, rather than making excuses.
- Praise and encourage team members who are working hard.
- Make criticisms constructively, and in private.
- Be assertive (put forward your point of view firmly) rather than aggressive (attacking other people to defend yourself).

Some notes of caution about being a team leader

- Try to look pleasant and don't glare at people who interrupt you unexpectedly.
- Never talk about team members behind their backs.
- Don't gossip, exaggerate to make a point, spread rumours, speculate or tell lies.
- Don't expect to get your own way all the time – all good leaders back down on occasion.
- Never criticise any colleagues in front of other people. Speak to them in private and keep it constructive.

TOP TIP

Excellent ideas often come from quiet team members. Encourage everyone to make suggestions so that you don't overlook any valuable contributions.

Key points

- There are many benefits of working in a group or as a team. These include mutual support, companionship and the exchange of ideas.
- You will be expected to work co-operatively with other people at work, and during many course assignments.

- It isn't easy learning to be a team leader. Team leaders should be fair, consistent and pleasant to work with, as well as loyal and sensitive to the needs of team members.

Action points

1 Identify the role of teamwork in your area of study. Identify the team's goal and any factors you think will contribute towards its success.

2 Decide how you would handle each of the following difficult situations if you were the team leader. If you can, discuss your ideas with a friend in your class.
   a) The team needs to borrow a college video camera to record an event being held tonight. Your tutor tells you that the one you reserved last week is not working and the rest are out on loan.
   b) A member of your team has personal problems so you have given him less work to do. Now you've been accused of having favourites.
   c) A team member is constantly letting everyone down because of poor work and non-attendance at group meetings.
   d) Two team members have disagreed about how to do a task. You're not bothered how they do it as long as it gets done properly, and by the deadline.
   e) A team member becomes very aggressive whenever she is challenged in any way – no matter how mildly.

3 Identify someone who has inspired you because they've been an excellent leader. This could be someone you've met, a fictional character or a famous person. Note down what it is about them that impressed you.

TOP TIP

Team working and bouncing ideas around produce quicker and better results than working in isolation.

Activity: Team roles

By applying teamwork principles to a design project, answer these questions. Remember that there will be different contexts for specialist activities, but inherently the core roles, responsibilities and purpose are generic.

1 What are the strongest skills that I can bring to a team?

2 How can I be a useful team member? (List four ways in which you can be useful.)

  i)

  ii)

  iii)

  iv)

3 How can I record my experience of working in teams?

4 What would I do if a team member dropped out because of illness or any other reason?

5 What would I do if the client we're working for doesn't like our ideas?

TOP TIPS

Remember when you are part of a team, you will have to find a balance between the team's needs and your own needs.

Step Eight: Understand how to research and analyse information

Case study: Efficient storage

Given the volume of research information that you will gather, efficient storage of matieral is crucial to your studies. It must therefore be carefully considered as you begin your BTEC National in Art and Design.

Gabriela's group realised early on that every aspect of learning on their course involved researching and recording evidence in one form or another.

Their tutor explains that organising research material would help achieve effective results as:

1 research without recording was only half of the activity

2 research requires analysis, evaluation and (possibly) action.

Gabriela's class organises a group discussion to see if they could establish some useful pointers and mechanisms for helping them to conduct their art and design research effectively and productively. They start by making a list of the research they might undertake on the course.

Contextual research: researching into the work of other artists and designers and researching into historical periods in art and design.

Techniques and processes research: researching into the physical processes (methods) used in art and design and researching to develop a basic understanding of specialist processes in art and design.

Visual research: researching for ideas development and producing visual evidence (2D/3D).

Activity-related research: recording evidence gathered during field trips and gallery and exhibition visits that could be of value during Level 3 creative studies.

All this research could be recorded in writing (notes), visually (in sketchbooks, photographs and videos), and by collecting samples and literature (for logbooks).

Reflection points

Think about how you can plan your research.

Decide how you are going to organise your research and whether you need to analyse the material. Ask your tutor for advice, if you're not sure how to proceed.

As a BTEC Level 3 National learner, you often have to find information for yourself. This skill will be invaluable in your working life and if you continue your studies at higher education level. Sometimes the information will give you a better understanding of a topic, at other times you will research information for a project or assignment. Sometimes you may be so interested in something that you want to find out more without being told to do so!

Whatever your reason, and no matter where your information can be found, there is a good and not-so-good way to go about the task. This section will help if you can't find what you want, or find too much, or drift aimlessly around a library, or watch a demonstration and don't know what to ask afterwards.

Types of information

There are many types of information and many different sources. Depending on the task, these are the sources you may need to consult.

- **Verbal information.** This includes talking to friends, colleagues at work and members of your family, listening to experts explain what they do, interviewing people, talking to sales reps at an exhibition or customers about a product.
- **Printed information**. This includes information printed in newspapers, journals, magazines, books, posters, workshop manuals, leaflets and catalogues. The type of magazine or newspaper you read may have its own slant on the information, which you may have to take into account.
- **Written information**. This includes course notes and handouts, reports, and other documents in the workplace. If you want to use written information from work, you must check that this is allowed and that it doesn't contain confidential material such as financial information or staff names and addresses.
- **Graphical information.** This includes illustrations, pictures, cartoons, line drawings, graphs and photographs. Graphics can make something clearer than words alone. For example, a satnav instruction book might contain illustrations to show different procedures.
- **Electronic information.** This includes information from electronic sources such as DVDs, CD-ROMs, searchable databases, websites, podcasts, webinars (**seminars** online), emails and text messages. The huge amount of information available online is both a help and a hindrance. You can find information quickly, but the source may be unreliable, out of date, inaccurate or inappropriate (see page 66.)

TOP TIP

Too much information is as bad as too little, because it's overwhelming. The trick is to find good-quality, relevant information and know when to call a halt to your search.

TOP TIP

Consider all appropriate sources and don't just rely on information found online.

Finding what you need

Spend a few minutes planning what to do before you start looking for information. This can save a lot of time later on.

The following steps will help you to do this.

1 Make sure you understand exactly what it is you need to know so that you don't waste time looking for the wrong thing.

2 Clarify your objectives to narrow down your search. Think about why the information is wanted and how much detail you need. For example, learners studying BTEC Nationals in Engineering and Performing Arts may both be researching 'noise' for their projects, but they are likely to need different types of information and use it in different ways.

3 Identify your sources and check you know how to use them. You need to choose sources that are most likely to provide information relevant to your objectives. For example, an engineering learner might find information on noise emissions in industry journals and by checking out specialist websites.

4 Plan and schedule your research. Theoretically, you could research information forever. Knowing when to call a halt takes skill. Write a schedule that states when you must stop looking and start sorting the information.

5 Store your information safely in a labelled folder. This folder should include printouts or photocopies of articles, notes about events you have attended or observed, photographs you've taken or sketches you've drawn. Divide your information under topic headings to make it easier to find. When you're ready to start work, re-read your assignment brief and select the items that are most closely related to the task you are doing.

TOP TIP

Allocate time for research as part of your assignment task. Take into account any interim deadlines as well as the final deadline for completing the work.

Primary and secondary research, and the law of copyright

There are two ways to research information. One is known as primary research, the other is secondary research.

Primary research

Primary research involves finding new information about an issue or topic. This might include finding out people's views about a product or interviewing an expert. When carrying out interviews, you will need to design a survey or questionnaire. Your primary research might also include observing or experiencing something for yourself, and recording your feelings and observations.

Secondary research

Secondary research involves accessing information that already exists in books, files and newspapers or on CD-ROMs, computer databases or the internet, and assessing it against your objectives.

This information has been prepared by other people and is available to anyone. You can quote from an original work provided you acknowledge the source of your information. You should put this acknowledgement in your text or in the bibliography to your text; do not claim it as your own research. You must include the author's name, year of publication, the title and publisher, or the web address if it is an online article. You should practise listing the sources of articles so

that you feel confident writing a bibliography. Use the guidance sheet issued by your centre to help you. This will illustrate the style your centre recommends.

The trick with research is to choose the best technique to achieve your objectives, and this may mean using a mix of methods and resources. For example, if you have to comment on an industry event you might go to it, make notes, interview people attending, observe the event (perhaps take a video camera), and read any newspaper reports or online comments.

TOP TIP

Always make sure you make a note of where you get information from (your source). Keep it safely as it can be very difficult later on to work out where it came from!

People as a source of information

If you want to get the most out of interviewing someone or several people, you need to prepare carefully in advance.

The following points give some general advice about getting the most out of face-to-face interviews.

- Make sure you know what questions to ask to get the information you need.
- Explain why you want the information.
- Don't expect to be told confidential or sensitive information.
- Write clear notes so that you remember who told you what, and when. (See also page 68.)
- Note the contact details of the person you are interviewing and ask whether they mind if you contact them again should you think of anything later or need to clarify your notes.
- Thank them for their help.

If you want to ask a lot of people for their opinion, you may want to conduct a survey. You will need to design a questionnaire and analyse the results. This will be easier if you ask for **quantitative** responses – for example yes/no, true/false or ratings on a five-point scale – rather than opinions.

- Give careful thought to your representative sample (people whose opinions are relevant to the topic).
- Decide how many people to survey so that the results mean something.
- Keep the survey relatively short.

- Thank people who complete it.
- Analyse the results, and write up your conclusions promptly.

TOP TIP

Test your questionnaire on volunteers before you 'go live' to check that there are no mistakes and that the questions are easy to understand. Make any amendments before you conduct your 'real' survey.

Asking someone who knows a lot about a topic can be informative.

Avoiding pitfalls

Wikipedia is a good online source that covers many topics, and often in some depth. It is popular and free. However, it has an open-content policy, which means that anyone can contribute to and edit entries. People may post information whether it is correct or not. Wikipedia is moving towards greater checks on entries, but it is still sensible to check out information you find on this site somewhere else.

Apart from inaccuracy, there are other problems that you may find with any information you obtain through research, especially material found online.

- **Out-of-date material.** Check the date of everything and keep only the latest version of books, newspapers or magazines. Yesterday's news may be of little use if you are researching something topical.
- **Irrelevant details.** Often, only part of an article will be relevant to your search. For example, if you are forecasting future trends in an area of work, you do not need information about its history or related problems. When learners are struggling, they sometimes 'pad out' answers with irrelevant information. If you've researched properly you can avoid this by having enough relevant information for your purposes.

- **Invalid assumptions.** This means someone has jumped to the wrong conclusion and made 2 + 2 = 5. You might do this if you see two friends chatting and think they are talking about you – whether they are or not! You can avoid problems in this area by double-checking your ideas and getting evidence to support them.

- **Bias.** This is when people hold strong views about a topic, or let their emotions or prejudices affect their judgement. An obvious example is asking a keen football fan for an objective evaluation of their team's performance!

- **Vested interests.** People may argue in a certain way because it's in their own interests to do so. For example, when the government said Home Information Packs must be prepared for all properties being sold, the Association of Home Information Pack Providers was in favour because it trains the people who prepare the packs. The National Association of Estate Agents and Royal Institution of Chartered Surveyors were not, because they thought they would lose business if people were put off selling their houses.

TOP TIP

Don't discard information that is affected by bias or vested interests. Just make it clear you know about the problem and have taken it into account.

Reading for a purpose

You may enjoy reading or you may find it tedious or difficult. If so, it helps to know that there are different ways to read, depending on what you're doing. For example, you wouldn't look for a programme in a TV guide in the same way that you would check an assignment for mistakes. You can save time and find information more easily if you use the best method of reading to suit your purpose. The following are some examples of ways of reading.

- **Skim reading** is used to check new information and get a general overview.
  To skim a book chapter, read the first and last paragraphs, the headings, subheadings and illustrations. It also helps to read the first sentence of each paragraph.

TOP TIP

News articles are written with the key points at the beginning, so concentrate on the first paragraph or two. Feature articles have a general introduction and important information is contained in the main text.

- **Scanning** is used to see whether an article contains something you need – such as key words, dates or technical terms.
  Focus on capital or initial letters for a name, and figures for a date. Technical terms may be in bold or italics.

- **Light reading** is usually done for pleasure when you are relaxed, for example, reading a magazine article. You may not remember many facts afterwards, so this sort of reading isn't suitable for learning something or assessing its value.

- **Word-by-word reading (proofreading)** is important so that you don't miss anything, such as the dosage instructions for a strong medicine. You should proofread assignments before you submit them.

- **Reading for study (active reading)** means being actively involved so that you understand the information. It is rare to be naturally good at this, so you might have to work to develop this skill.

Developing critical and analytical skills

Developing critical and analytical skills involves looking at information for any flaws in the arguments. These skills are important when you progress to work or higher education (HE), so it's useful to practise them now on your BTEC Level 3 National course.

A useful technique for understanding, analysing, evaluating and remembering what you are reading is **SQ4R**.

SQ4R is an effective method. It consists of six steps.

1 Survey first, to get a general impression. Scan the information to see what it is about, when it was written and by whom. The source, and the reason it was written, may be important. Most newspapers, for example, have their own 'slant' that affects how information is presented.

2 Question your aims for reading this material. What are you hoping to find? What questions are you expecting it to answer?

3 Read the information three or four times. The first time, aim to get a general idea of the content. Use a dictionary to look up any new words. Then read more carefully to really understand what the writer means.

4 Respond by thinking critically about the information and how it relates to the topic you are studying. Does it answer your queries partially, fully or not at all? What information is factual and what is based on opinion? Is there evidence to support these opinions? Is there a reason why the author has taken this standpoint? Do you agree with it? How does it link to other information you have read? What is the opposite argument and is there any evidence to support this? Overall, how useful is this information?

5 Record the information by noting the key points. Use this to refresh your memory, if necessary, rather than re-reading the article.

6 Review your notes against the original to check you have included all important points. If you are also preparing a presentation, reviewing your notes will help you to remember key points more easily.

TOP TIP

SQ4R is just one method of reading for study. Research others and adapt them to suit your own style.

Taking good notes

There are many occasions when you need to take notes, such as when a visiting speaker is talking to your class. There's no point taking notes unless you write them in a way that will allow you to use them later.

Note-taking is a personal activity. Some people prefer to make diagrammatical sketches with key points in boxes linked by arrows, others prefer to write a series of bullet points. You will develop your own style, but the following hints and tips might help you at the start.

- Use A4 lined paper, rather than a notebook, so that you have more space and don't need to turn over so often.
- When you're reading for study, make sure you have a dictionary, pen, notepad and highlighter to hand.
- Leave a wide margin to record your own comments or queries.
- Put a heading at the top, such as the speaker's name and topic, as well as the date.
- If you are making notes from a book or an article, remember SQ4R and read it several times first. Your notes will only be effective if you understand the information.
- Don't write in complete sentences – it takes too long.
- Leave spaces for later additions or corrections.
- Use headings to keep your notes clear and well organised.
- Only write down relevant information, including key words and phrases.

- Highlight, underline or use capitals for essential points.
- Never copy chunks of text – always use your own words.
- Clearly identify quotations, and record your sources, so that you can cite them in your work. (Note the author's name, title of the work, publisher, date and place of publication and the page number.)

TOP TIP

Make sure your information is accurate, up to date, relevant and valid. Be aware of bias, and don't confuse fact with opinion.

Key points

- Useful information may be verbal, printed, written, graphical or electronic.
- Effective research means knowing exactly what you are trying to find and where to look. Know how reference media are stored in your library and how to search online. Store important information carefully.
- Primary research is original data you obtain yourself. Secondary research is information prepared by someone else. If you use this, you must quote your sources in a bibliography.
- You can search for information by skimming and scanning, and read in different ways. Reading for study means actively involving yourself with the text, questioning what you are reading and making notes to help your own understanding.
- Read widely around a topic to get different viewpoints. Don't accept everything you read as correct. Think about how it fits with other information you have obtained.
- Taking notes is a personal skill that takes time to develop. Start by using A4 lined pages with a margin, set out your notes clearly and label them. Only record essential information.

Action points

- Working with a friend, look back at the sources of information listed on page 32. For each type, identify examples of information relevant to your course that you could obtain from each source. See how many you can list under each type.
- Check your ability to find the information you need by answering each of the questions in **Activity: Finding information** on the next page. For any questions you get wrong, your first research task is to find out the correct answers as quickly as you can.
- Go to page 96 to find out how you can access a website where you can check your ability to skim and scan information, improve your ability to differentiate fact from opinion, summarise text, and much more.
- Check your ability to sort fact from opinion and spot vested interests by completing **Activity: Let's give you a tip…** on page 72. Check your ideas with the answers on page 95.

TOP TIP

Make a note of any information that you are struggling to understand so that you can discuss it with your tutor.

Activity: Finding information

Answer the following questions about finding information.

a) Four types of information that are available from the library in your centre, besides books, are:

1

2

3

4

b) When I visit the library, the way to check if a book I want is available is:

c) The difference between borrowing a book on short-term loan and on long-term loan is:

Short-term loan:

Long-term loan:

d) The journals that are stocked by the library that are relevant to my course include:

e) Useful information on the intranet at my centre includes:

f) Searchable databases and online magazines I can access include:

g) The quickest way to check if a book or journal contains the type of information I need is to:

h) The difference between a search engine, a portal, a directory site and a forum is:

i) Bookmarking useful websites means:

j) In addition to suggesting websites, Google can also provide the following types of information:

k) Specialist websites which provide useful information related to my course include:

l) Useful tips I would give to people starting on my course who need to find out information are:

Activity: Let's give you a tip...

In 2009 many businesses were struggling, thanks to the credit crunch and falling consumer demand. Some, like Woolworths, closed down altogether. Others laid off staff, or announced wage cuts. Despite this, the government approved recommendations by the Low Pay Commission to increase the minimum wage rate from October. Although the rise was only small, many unions, including Unison and Usdaw, agreed it was better than a freeze, which had been wanted by the British Chambers of Commerce and the British Retail Consortium.

The government also announced new laws to stop restaurants and bars using tips to top up staff pay to the minimum level. *The Independent* newspaper claimed its 'fair tips, fair pay' campaign had won the day. It also reported that the British Hospitality Association was claiming this could result in up to 45,000 job losses. The Unite union also carried out a campaign, and its General Secretary claimed the decision a triumph for the poorly paid. Not everyone agreed. Some thought there should be no tipping at all, as in Australia. Others said the Canadian system was best – wages are low but generous tips are left, and this motivates staff to give excellent service.

a) Look at the table below. In your view, which of the statements are facts and which are opinions? In each case, justify your view.

Statement	Fact or opinion?	Justification
i) Having a national minimum wage helps low-paid workers.		
ii) Over one million people will benefit from the minimum wage increase.		
iii) The new law on tips will stop restaurants paying below minimum wage rates.		
iv) Using the Australian system of no tips would be better.		
v) The Canadian system guarantees good service.		
vi) 45,000 job losses will occur in the hospitality industry.		

b) All newspapers have their own way of putting forward the news. Go to page 96 to find out how you can access a website which will help you to compare the way that news is reported in different newspapers.

Compare six different newspapers and make notes on:
i) the type of stories covered

ii) the way views are put forward.

Activity: Organising research materials

Mind mapping is one way of organising research material. Go to page 96 to access a useful website about using mind maps in this way. Once research is complete, the mind map can be extended to include analysis and evaluation.

Use the space below to create your own mind map – be creative and make it look as interesting as you can. Your mind map may cover these research methods:

- ideas development and experimentation
- surveys and questionnaires
- observation of people, places or other artwork.

TOP TIPS

Search for mind mapping resources online; some have fantastic graphics!

Step Nine: Make an effective presentation

Presentation is one of the keys to success, and nowhere more so than in art and design, as the learners in Ashley's BTEC National group are quickly finding out. The learners quickly realise that if they can not present their evidence clearly and succinctly, they are potentially missing out on higher grading levels. Their design proposals might be brilliant and unique, but this counts for little if they are not presented poperly. It isn't just about how well they could draw or paint, but also about how cleverly they present their visual ideas.

Ashley's tutor explains that the group is going to work on a project to introduce 3D and textile installations in the local NHS hospital's children's waiting area. Ashley and his fellow learners are reminded that the work will be assessed in the usual way for their BTEC Level 3 National in Art and Design. The client (the local NHS hospital) will complete a witness testimony, which will provide evidence towards some unit grading criteria.

During the project briefing, Ashley's tutor tells the group that when they are preparing their presentations they should concentrate on the key factors of making presentations. They should think about what it is that they are going to present, how they will present it and how their audience will react.

Reflection points

How will you prepare for any presentations you will make?

Can you name two critical elements of team presentation?

Making a presentation can be nerve-wracking. It involves several skills, including planning, preparation and communication. It tests your ability to work in a team, speak in public and use IT (normally PowerPoint). You also have to stay calm under pressure. However, as it is excellent practice for your future, you can expect presentations to be a common method of assessing your performance.

TOP TIP

When you're giving a presentation, keep to time, get to the point and use your time well.

Good planning and preparation

Being well prepared, and rehearsing beforehand, helps your confidence and your presentation. The following points will help you to do this.

- If you're part of a team, find out everyone's strengths and weaknesses and divide work fairly, taking these into account. Decide how long each person should speak, who should introduce the team and who will summarise at the end.

- Take into account the time you have been allocated, your resources and team skills. A simple, clear presentation is better – and safer – than a complicated one.

- If you're using PowerPoint, make slides more interesting by avoiding a series of bulleted lists and including artwork. Print PowerPoint notes for the audience. Use a fuller set of notes for yourself, as a prompt.

- Check the venue and time.

- Decide what to wear and check it's clean and presentable.

- Prepare, check and print your handouts.

- Decide, as a team, the order in which people will speak, bearing in mind the topic.

- Discuss possible questions and how to answer them.

- Rehearse beforehand to check your timings.

If you prepare properly, you can really enjoy giving a presentation.

TOP TIP

Rehearsing properly allows you to speak fluently, just glancing at your notes to remind you of the next key point.

On the day, you can achieve a better performance if you:

- arrive in plenty of time
- calm your nerves by taking deep breaths before going in front of your audience
- introduce yourself clearly, and smile at the audience
- avoid reading from your screen or your notes
- explain what you are going to do – especially if giving a demonstration – do it, and then review what you've done
- say you will deal with questions at the end of any demonstration
- answer questions honestly – don't exaggerate, guess or waffle
- respond positively to all feedback, which should be used to improve your performance next time.

TOP TIPS

Make sure you can be heard clearly by lifting your head and speaking a little more slowly and loudly than normal.

Key points

- When making a presentation, prepare well, don't be too ambitious, and have several rehearsals.
- When giving a demonstration, explain first what you are going to do and that you will answer questions at the end.

Case study: Learner quotes about making presentations

Most people start off feeling uncomfortable about talking in front of a group of people, whether you know them or not. This is what some real learners have said about having to give presentations as part of their BTEC course.

'I used to dread presentations on my course, but found that if I went through my notes again and again until I knew the presentation inside out, it made it much easier and the presentations generally went well.'

Javinder, 17, BTEC Level 3 National in Construction

'I used to be petrified of talking in front of other people but over time I've learned that, if I prepare well before a presentation, I usually feel much more confident on the day. If I know my material, I don't have to look down at my notes all the time and can make eye contact with the audience. Taking a few deep breaths before I begin keeps me calm and allows me to focus.'

Katie, 19, BTEC Level 3 National in Creative Media Production

'I used to hate presenting to other people on my course, until I realised that most of them were as nervous about it as I was!'

Koichi, 21, BTEC Level 3 National in Art and Design

'Less is more! I used to rely on props and, as I was nervous about forgetting things or running out of things to say, I talked far too quickly. I had to repeat everything as nobody knew what I was on about! Some of my best presentations have been done without using slides or any other props at all, just talking (slowly of course) to my audience.'

Laura, 18, BTEC Level 3 National in Health & Social Care

'I prefer to be assessed by oral presentations as I'm dyslexic and my written work lets me down all the time. Everyone tells me that I really shine and show that I know my stuff when I present it to the rest of the group.'

Sam, 17, BTEC Level 3 National in Business

Activity: All right on the night?

Read the following account and answer the questions that follow.
If possible, compare ideas with a friend in your class.

Gemma looked around in exasperation. The team were on the final rehearsal of their presentation and nothing was going right. Amaya seemed to think it was funny. 'Honestly, Gemma, why don't you just chill for a bit?' she suggested. 'You know what they say – a bad dress rehearsal means we'll do really well tomorrow!'

Gemma glared at her. 'Well, can I make a suggestion, too, Amaya,' she retorted. 'Why don't you just concentrate for a change? Sprawling around and dissolving into giggles every five minutes isn't helping either.'

She turned to Adam. 'And I thought you were going to build a simple model,' she said, 'not one that falls apart every time you touch it.'

Adam looked crestfallen. 'But I wanted to show how it worked.'

'How it's supposed to work, you mean!' raged Gemma, all her worries and anxieties now coming to the fore. 'We'll look stupid if it ends up in bits on the floor tomorrow and Amaya just falls about laughing again.'

'And Imran,' continued Gemma, turning her sights on the last member of the team, 'why is it so difficult for you to count to three minutes? We've agreed over and over again we'll each talk for three minutes, and every time you get carried away with the sound of your own voice and talk for twice as long. It just means we're going to overrun and get penalised. And stop trying to wriggle out of answering questions properly. For heaven's sake, if you don't know the answer, how hard is it just to say so?'

Silence fell. No one looked at each other. Adam fiddled with his model and something else fell off. Amaya wanted to laugh but didn't dare to do so.

Imran was sulking and vowed never to say anything ever again. 'You wait,' he thought. 'Tomorrow I'll race through my part in one minute flat. And then you'll be sorry, you won't know what to do.'

1 Identify the strengths and weaknesses of each member of the presentation team.

Name	Strengths	Weaknesses
Gemma		
Amaya		
Adam		
Imran		

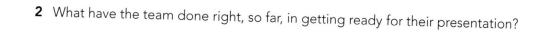

2 What have the team done right, so far, in getting ready for their presentation?

3 Why do you think they are having problems?

4 If you were Gemma's tutor, what advice would you give her at this point?

Activity: Presentation checklist

Work in teams of four to produce a proposal for some new informational graphics for the waiting area of medical drop-in centres that explain community support services. You will be responsible for the presentation of the design proposals produced by the design team to the judging panel.

The table below lists some key strategies for making effective presentations. You need to provide detailed actions in the blank column, based on the above scenario. It will help if your team visits a local medical centre to look at current information displays – this may give you some ideas of how you could present this work.

Aim to feel confident by being knowledgeable about your team's proposals	
Use proven presentation techniques to promote your team's design proposals	
Use simple and relevant language in presenting your team's design proposals	
Design a strategy for engaging audience interest from the start	
Plan the presentation to maximise impact, attention and appreciation	

TOP TIPS

When making a PowerPoint presentation, don't just read out what it says on the slides. The audience can do this. Use the slides as prompt cards.

Step Ten: Maximise your opportunities and manage your problems

Case study: Maximising your potential

Lauren has always been interested in textiles, graphics and product design at school. She had a career review during her exit year at secondary where she realised that she wanted to consider further studies in art and design. She had previously felt uncertain about which academic route, if any, she wanted to follow and which potential career pathway she might choose. Her career adviser has arranged for her to visit the art department at a local further education college.

In speaking to the students on the BTEC National in Art and Design, she is keen to hear about the way they studied. She learns about assignment-based delivery and the assessment process with grades of pass, merit and distinction, and looks at some portfolio work across all of these grading levels. The tutor explains that a BTEC National in Art and Design provides opportunities to work at a pace and in a style suited to the individual, albeit within given timescales, and that the course and its assessment strategy is structured to allow for continual improvement. Lauren feels really positive about this as she has always worked at an average pace but lacked confidence about her own skills potential. Jack, a student, shows her an assignment brief and the work that he

had produced in response. She looks at his tutor's feedback and is encouraged by the direction given on what he should do to attain higher grading levels.

The tutor chats to Lauren about the assessment process, explaining how it is structured and how feedback is used to recognise weaknesses and identify areas for improvement. The course itself allows for the development of general and specialist skills. The tutor tells her that it is a great course on which to develop work-based competences that could eventually lead to a full-time career in art and design. Lauren is able to get some positive answers to all her questions.

Will this course build my confidence and self-esteem?

Will I develop new skills?

Will I become a successful designer?

Reflection points

What do you think?

Are there any aspects of the course that you feel you need to know more about?

If your course takes one or two years to complete, then it is highly likely that you will experience some highs and lows in that time. You may find one or two topics harder than the rest. There may be distractions in your personal life to cope with. All of this means that you may not always be able to do your best.

It is, therefore, sensible to have an action plan to help you cope. It's also wise to plan how to make the best of opportunities for additional

experiences or learning. This section shows you how to do this.

TOP TIP

Because life rarely runs smoothly, it's sensible to capitalise on the opportunities that come your way and have a plan to deal with problems.

Making the most of your opportunities

There will be many opportunities for learning on your course, not all of which will be in school or college. You should prepare for some of the following to maximise the opportunities that each offers.

- **External visits**. Prepare in advance by reading about relevant topics. Make notes when you are there. Write up your notes neatly and file them safely for future reference.

- **Visiting speakers**. Questions can usually be submitted to the speaker in advance. Think carefully about information that you would find helpful. Make notes, unless someone has been appointed to make notes for the whole group. You may be asked to thank the speaker on behalf of your group.

- **Work experience**. If work experience is an essential part of your course, your tutor will help you to organise your placement and tell you about the evidence you need to obtain. You may also get a special logbook in which to record your experiences. Read and re-read the units to which your evidence will apply, and make sure you understand the grading criteria and what you need to obtain. Make time to write up your notes, logbook and/or diary every night (if possible), while everything is fresh in your mind.

- **In your own workplace**. If you have a full-time or part-time job, watch for opportunities to find out more about relevant topics that relate to your course, such as health and safety, teamwork, dealing with customers, IT security and communications. Your employer will have had to address all of these issues. Finding out more about these issues will broaden your knowledge and give more depth to your assessment responses.

- **Television, newspapers, podcasts and other information sources**. The media can be an invaluable source of information. Look out for news bulletins relating to your studies, as well as information in topical television programmes – from *The Apprentice* to *Top Gear*. You can also read news headlines online (see page 96). Podcasts are useful, too. It will help if you know what topics you will be studying in the months to come, so you can spot useful opportunities as they arise.

TOP TIP

Remember that you can use online catch-up services, such as the BBC iPlayer or 4oD (for Channel 4 shows) to see TV programmes you have missed recently.

Minimising problems

Hopefully, any problems you experience during your course will only be minor, such as struggling to find an acceptable working method with someone in your team.

You should already know who to talk to about these issues, and who to go to if that person is absent or you would prefer to talk to someone else. If your problems are affecting your work, it's sensible to see your tutor promptly. It is a rare learner who is enthusiastic about every topic and gets on well with everyone else doing the course, so your tutor won't be surprised and will give you useful guidance (in confidence) to help.

TOP TIP

Don't delay talking to someone in confidence if you have a serious problem. If your course tutor is unavailable, talk to another staff member instead.

Other sources of help

If you are unfortunate enough to have a more serious personal problem, the following sources of help may be available in your centre.

- **Professional counselling.** There may be a professional counselling service. If you see a counsellor, nothing you say during the session can be mentioned to another member of staff without your permission.

- **Complaint procedures.** If you have a serious complaint, the first step is to talk to your tutor. If you can't resolve your problem informally, there will be a formal learner complaint procedure. These procedures are used only for serious issues, not for minor difficulties.

- **Appeals procedures.** If you disagree with your final grade for an assignment, check the grading criteria and ask the subject tutor to explain how the grade was awarded. If you are still unhappy, talk to your personal tutor. If you still disagree, you have the right to make a formal appeal.

- **Disciplinary procedures.** These exist for when learners consistently flout a centre's rules, and ensure that all learners are dealt with in the same way. Hopefully, you will never get into trouble, but you should make sure that you read these procedures carefully to see what could happen if you did. Remember that being honest and making a swift apology is always the wisest course of action.

- **Serious illness.** Whether this involves you, a family member or a close friend, it could affect your attendance. Discuss the problem with your tutor promptly; you will be missing information from the first day you are absent. There are many solutions in this type of situation – such as sending notes by post and updating you electronically (providing you are well enough to cope with the work).

TOP TIP

It's important to know your centre's procedures for dealing with important issues such as complaints, major illnesses, learner appeals and disciplinary matters.

Key points

- Don't miss opportunities to learn more about relevant topics through external visits, listening to visiting speakers, work experience, being at work or even watching television.

- If you have difficulties or concerns, talk to your tutor, or another appropriate person, promptly to make sure your work isn't affected.

Action points

1 Prepare in advance to maximise your opportunities.

   a) List the opportunities available on your course for obtaining more information and talking to experts. You can check with your tutor to make sure you've identified them all.

   b) Check the content of each unit you will be studying so that you know the main topics and focus of each.

   c) Identify the information that may be relevant to your course on television, on radio, in newspapers and in podcasts.

2 Make sure you know how to cope if you have a serious problem.

   a) Check your centre's procedures so you know who to talk to in a crisis, and who to contact if that person is absent.

   b) Find out where you can get hold of a copy of the main procedures in your centre that might affect you if you have a serious problem. Then read them.

Activity: Maximising your opportunities and minimising problems

Below is a simple diagram showing one way to plan solutions to a task. What is the key point the diagram is referring to? What are the potential solutions the diagram is referring to?

Taking one of your current assignment briefs, try and map the individual actions (devise, analyse, action etc) against the design-related activities identified in a current assignment brief. Use the blank template below for this task. This activity may help you to maximise your grade and to avoid potential pitfalls with timescales, problem-solving etc.

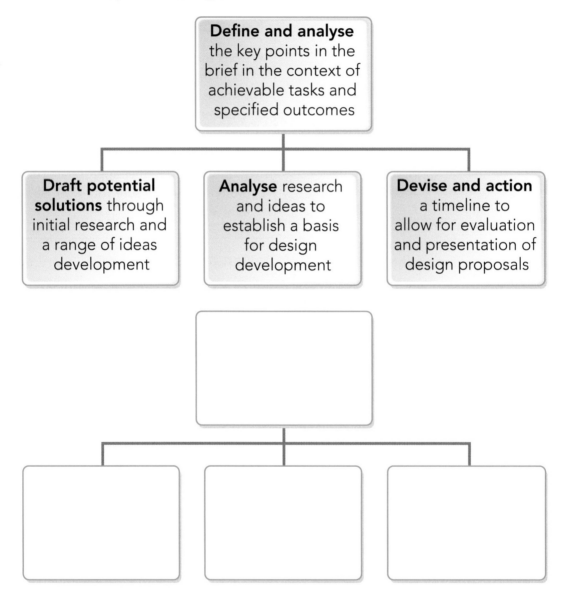

AND FINALLY ...

Refer to this Study Skills Guide whenever you need to remind yourself about something related to your course. Keep it in a safe place so that you can use it whenever you need to refresh your memory. That way, you'll get the very best out of your course – and yourself!

TOP TIP

The time and effort you will be putting into this course deserve to be rewarded. Make sure you know how to confront and successfully overcome problems.

Skills building

This section has been written to help you improve the skills needed to do your best in your assignments. You may be excellent at some skills already; others may need further work. The skills you can expect to demonstrate on your course include:

- your personal, learning and thinking skills (**PLTS**)
- your **functional skills** of ICT, maths/numeracy and English
- your proofreading and document production skills.

Personal, learning and thinking skills (PLTS)

These are the skills, personal qualities and behaviour that enable you to operate more independently, work more confidently with other people and be more effective at work. You'll develop these on your BTEC Level 3 National course through a variety of experiences and as you take on different roles and responsibilities.

The skills are divided into six groups.

1 **Independent enquirers** can process and evaluate information they investigate from different perspectives. They can plan what to do and how to do it, and take into account the consequences of making different decisions.

2 **Creative thinkers** generate and explore different ideas. They make connections between ideas, events and experiences that enable them to be inventive and imaginative.

3 **Reflective learners** can assess themselves and other people. They can evaluate their own strengths and limitations. They set themselves realistic goals, monitor their own performance and welcome feedback.

4 **Team workers** collaborate with other people to achieve common goals. They are fair and considerate to others, whether as a team leader or team member, and take account of different opinions.

5 **Self-managers** are well-organised and show personal responsibility, initiative, creativity and enterprise. They look for new challenges and responsibilities, and are flexible when priorities change.

6 **Effective participators** play a full part in the life of their school, college, workplace or wider community by taking responsible action to bring improvements for others as well as themselves.

Action points

1 Many parts of this Study Skills Guide relate to the development of your own personal, learning and thinking skills. For each of the following, suggest the main skill groups to which the chapter relates. Refer to the box above and write a number next to each chapter title below.

a) Use your time wisely. ____

b) Understand how to research and analyse information. ____

c) Work productively as a member of a group. ____

d) Understand yourself. ____

e) Utilise all your resources. ____

f) Maximise your opportunities and manage your problems. ____

2 You have been on your BTEC National course for a few months now and, although everyone is enjoying the work, you realise that some of the learners have complaints.

First, several learners object to an increase in the price of printouts and photocopying, on the basis that they can't do good work for their assignments if this is too expensive. You disagree and think that the prices are reasonable, given the cost of paper.

Second, a timetable change means your 2 pm – 4 pm Friday afternoon class has been moved to 9 am – 11 am. Some learners are annoyed and want it changed back, while others are delighted.

a) For the first problem, identify four factors which could indicate that those complaining about the price rise might be justified.

1

2

3

4

b) Now consider the second problem.

i) Think about which learners in your group would be most affected by the timetable change. Who might be most disturbed? Who might benefit from the earlier start?

ii) Try to think of a creative solution, or compromise, that would please both groups.

c) During the discussions about these issues, some quieter members of the class are often shouted down by the more excitable members. Suggest a strategy for dealing with this which everyone is likely to accept.

You can also check your ideas with the suggestions given on page 95.

3 a) Complete the chart opposite, identifying occasions when you may need to demonstrate personal, learning and thinking skills in your future career. Alternatively, apply each area to a part-time job you are currently doing.

b) Identify areas where you think you are quite strong and put a tick in the 'S' column. Check that you could provide evidence to support this judgement, such as a time when you have demonstrated this skill.

c) Now consider areas where you are not so good and put a cross in the 'W' column.

d) Then practise self-management by identifying two appropriate goals to achieve over the next month, and make a note of them in the space provided. If possible, talk through your ideas at your next individual tutorial.

Personal, learning and thinking skills for future career/current part-time job				
Skill group	**Example skills**	**Occasions when you use/ will use skill**	**S**	**W**
Independent enquirers	Finding information Solving problems Making decisions Reconciling conflicting information or views Justifying decisions			
Creative thinkers	Finding imaginative solutions Making original connections Finding new ways to do something Opportunities for being innovative and inventive			
Reflective learners	Goals you may set yourself Reviewing your own progress Encouraging feedback Dealing with setbacks or criticism			
Team workers	Working with others Coping with different views from your own Adapting your behaviour Being fair and considerate			
Self-managers	Being self-starting and showing initiative Dealing positively with changing priorities Organising your own time and resources Dealing with pressure Managing your emotions			
Effective participators	Identifying issues of concern to others Proposing ways forward Identifying improvements for others Influencing other people Putting forward a persuasive argument			
Goals	1			
	2			

Functional skills

Functional skills are practical skills that everyone needs to have in order to study and work effectively. They involve using and applying English, maths and ICT.

Improving your literacy skills

Your written English communication skills

A good vocabulary increases your ability to explain yourself clearly. Work that is presented without spelling and punctuation errors looks professional, and increases the likelihood of someone understanding your intended meaning. Your written communication skills will be tested in many assignments. You should work at improving areas of weakness, such as spelling, punctuation or vocabulary.

Try the following ideas to help you improve your written communication skills.

- Read more as this introduces you to new words, and it will help your spelling.
- Look up new words in a dictionary and try to use them in conversation.
- Use a thesaurus (you can access one electronically in Word) to find alternatives to words you use a lot; this adds variety to your work.
- Never use words you don't understand in the hope that they sound impressive.
- Write neatly, so people can read what you've written.
- Do crosswords to improve your word power and spelling.
- Improve your punctuation – especially the use of apostrophes – either by using an online programme or by using a communication textbook.
- Go to page 96 to find out how to gain access to some helpful websites for this page.

Verbal and non-verbal communication (NVC) skills

Talking appropriately means using the right words and 'tone'; using the right body language means sending positive signals to reinforce this message – such as smiling at someone when you say 'Hello'. Both verbal and non-verbal communication skills are essential when dealing with people at work.

The following ideas are some hints for successful communication.

- Be polite, tactful, and sensitive to other people's feelings.
- Think about the words and phrases that you like to hear, and use them when communicating with other people.
- Use simple language so that people can understand you easily. Explain what you mean, when necessary.
- Speak at the right pace. Don't speak so slowly that everyone loses interest, or so fast that no one can understand you.
- Speak loudly enough for people to hear you clearly – but don't shout!
- Think about the specific needs of different people – whether you are talking to a senior manager, an important client, a shy colleague or an angry customer.
- Recognise the importance of non-verbal communication (NVC) so that you send positive signals by smiling, making eye contact, giving an encouraging nod or leaning forwards to show interest.
- Read other people's body language to spot if they are anxious or impatient so that you can react appropriately.

TOP TIP

Make sure you use the right tone for the person you're talking to. Would you talk to an adult in the same way you'd talk to a very young child?

Action points

1 Go to page 96 to find out how to gain access to websites which can help you to improve your literacy skills.

2 A battery made in China contained the following information.

> **DO NOT CONNECT IMPROPERLY**
>
> **CHARGE OR DISPOSE OF IN FIRE**

a) Can you see any problems with this? Give a reason for your answer.

b) Reword the information so that it is unambiguous.

3 If you ever thought you could completely trust the spellchecker on your computer, type the text given in box A on the next page into your computer. Your spellchecker will not highlight a single error; yet even at a glance you should be able to spot dozens of errors!

Read the passage in box A (overleaf) and try to understand it. Then rewrite it in box B on the next page without spelling, grammatical or punctuation errors. Compare your finished work with the suggested version on page 95.

Box A

> Anyone desirable to write books or reports, be they short or long, should strive too maximise they're optimal use of one's English grammar and obliviously there is an need for correct spelling two one should not neglect punctuation neither.
>
> Frequent lea, many people and individuals become confusing or just do not no it, when righting, when words that mean different, when sounding identically, or when pronounced very similar, are knot too bee spelled inn the same whey. The quay two suck seeding is dew care, a lack off witch Leeds too Miss Spellings that mite otherwise of bean a voided. Spell chequers donut find awl missed takes.
>
> Despite all the pitfalls how ever, with practise, patients and the right altitude, any one can soon become a grate writer and speaker, as what I did.

Box B Now rewrite the passage in the space below without errors.

4 In each of the statements listed in the table below suggest what the body language described might mean.

Statement	What might this body language mean?
a) You are talking to your manager when he steps away from you and crosses his arms over his chest.	
b) You are talking to your friend about what she did at the weekend but she's avoiding making eye contact with you.	
c) During a tutorial session, your tutor is constantly tapping his fingers on the arm of his chair.	
d) Whenever you talk to your friend about your next assignment, she bites her lower lip.	

Improving your maths or numeracy skills

If you think numeracy isn't relevant to you, then think again! Numeracy is an essential life skill. If you can't carry out basic calculations accurately then you will have problems, perhaps when you least expect them. You'll often encounter numbers in various contexts – sometimes they will be correctly given, sometimes not. Unless you have a basic understanding about numeracy, you won't be able to tell the difference.

Good numeracy skills will improve your ability to express yourself, especially in assignments and at work. If you have problems, there are strategies that you can practise to help:

- Try to do basic calculations in your head, then check them on a calculator.
- Ask your tutor for help if important calculations give you problems.
- When you are using your computer, use the onscreen calculator (or a spreadsheet package) to do calculations.
- Investigate puzzle sites and brain training software, such as Dr Kageyama's Maths Training by Nintendo.

Action points

1 Go to page 96 to find out how to gain access to websites which can help you to improve your numeracy skills.

2 Try the following task with a friend or family member.

Each of you should write down 36 simple calculations in a list, eg

8×6, $19 - 8$, $14 + 6$.

Exchange lists. See who can answer the most calculations correctly in the shortest time.

3 Figures aren't always what they appear to be. For example, Sophie watches *Who Wants To Be a Millionaire?* She hears Chris Tarrant say

that there have been over 500 shows, with 1200 contestants who have each won over £50,000 on average. Five people have won £1 million.

Sophie says she is going to enter because she is almost certain to win more than £50,000 and could even win a million pounds.

a) On the figures given, what is the approximate total of money won over 500 shows (to the nearest £ million)?

b) Assuming that Sophie is chosen to appear on the show, and makes it on air as a contestant, do you think Sophie's argument that she will 'almost certainly' win more than £50,000 is correct? Give a reason for your answer.

(The correct answer is on page 96.)

4 You have a part-time job and have been asked to carry out a survey on the usage of the drinks vending machine. You decide to survey 500 people, and find that:
- 225 use the machine to buy one cup of coffee per day only
- 100 use the machine to buy one cup of tea per day only
- 75 use the machine to buy one cup of cold drink per day only
- 50 use the machine to buy one cup of hot chocolate per day only
- the rest are non-users
- the ratio of male to female users is 2:1.

a) How many men in your survey use the machine?

b) How many women in your survey use the machine?

c) Calculate the proportion of the people in your survey that use the machine.

Express this as a fraction and as a percentage.

d) What is the ratio of coffee drinkers to tea drinkers in your survey?

e) What is the ratio of coffee drinkers to hot chocolate drinkers in your survey?

f) If people continue to purchase from the machine in the same ratio found in your survey, and last month 1800 cups of coffee were sold, what would you expect the sales of the cold drinks to be?

g) Using the answer to f), if coffee costs 65p and all cold drinks cost 60p, how much would have been spent in total last month on these two items?

Improving your ICT skills

Good ICT skills are an asset in many aspects of your daily life and not just for those studying to be IT practitioners.

These are ways in which you can improve your ICT skills.

- Check that you can use the main features of the software packages you need to produce your assignments, eg Word, Excel and PowerPoint.
- Choose a good search engine and learn to use it properly. For more information, go to page 96 to find out how to access a useful website.
- Developing and using your IT skills enables you to enhance your assignments. This may include learning how to import and export text and artwork from one package to another, taking digital photographs and inserting them into your work, and/or creating drawings or diagrams by using appropriate software.

Action points

1 Check your basic knowledge of IT terminology by identifying each of these items on your computer screen:

a) taskbar	**f)** scroll bars
b) toolbar	**g)** status bar
c) title bar	**h)** insertion point
d) menu bar	**i)** maximise/
e) mouse pointer	minimise button.

2 Assess your IT skills by identifying the packages and operations you find easy to use and those that you find more difficult. If you use Microsoft Office products (Word, PowerPoint, Access or Excel) you can find out more about improving your skills online. Go to page 96 to find out how to access a useful website for this action points section.

3 Search the internet to find a useful dictionary of IT terms. Bookmark it for future use. Find out the meaning of any of the following terms that you don't know already:

a) portal

b) cached link

c) home page

d) browser

e) firewall

f) HTML

g) URL

h) cookie

i) hyperlink

j) freeware.

Proofreading and document preparation skills

Improving your keyboard, document production and general IT skills can save you hours of time. When you have good skills, the work you produce will be of a far more professional standard.

* Think about learning to touch-type. Your centre may have a workshop you can join, or you can use an online program – go to page 96 to find out how to access a web link for this section. From here you can access websites that will allow you to test and work on improving your typing skills.

* Obtain correct examples of any document formats you will have to use, such as a report or summary, either from your tutor, from the internet or from a textbook.

* Proofread all your work carefully. A spellchecker won't find all your mistakes, so you must read through it yourself as well.

* Make sure your work looks professional by using a suitable typeface and font size, as well as reasonable margins.

* Print your work and store the printouts neatly, so that it stays in perfect condition for when you hand it in.

Action points

1 You can check and improve your typing skills using online typing sites – see link in previous section.

2 Check your ability to create documents by scoring yourself out of 5 for each of the following questions, where 5 is something you can do easily and 0 is something you can't do at all. Then focus on improving every score where you rated yourself 3 or less.

I know how to:

a) create a new document and open a saved document _____

b) use the mouse to click, double-click and drag objects _____

c) use drop-down menus _____

d) customise my toolbars by adding or deleting options _____

e) save and/or print a document _____

f) create folders and sub-folders to organise my work _____

g) move a folder I use regularly to My Places _____

h) amend text in a document _____

i) select, copy, paste and delete information in a document _____

j) quickly find and replace text in a document _____

k) insert special characters _____

l) create a table or insert a diagram in a document _____

m) change the text size, font and colour _____

n) add bold, italics or underscore _____

o) create a bullet or numbered list _____

p) align text left, right or centred _____

q) format pages before they are printed _____

r) proofread a document so that there are no mistakes _____.

Answers

Activity: Let's give you a tip... (page 72)

a) i) Fact
   ii) Opinion – the number cannot be validated
   iii) Fact
   iv) Opinion
   v) Opinion
   vi) Opinion – again the number is estimated

Skills building answers

PLTS action points (page 85)

1 a) Use your time wisely = **5** Self-managers
   b) Understand how to research and analyse information = **1** Independent enquirers, **5** Self-managers
   c) Work productively as a member of a group = **4** Team workers, **6** Effective participators
   d) Understand yourself = **3** Reflective learners
   e) Utilise all your resources = **5** Self-managers
   f) Maximise your opportunities and manage your problems = **1** Independent enquirers, **2** Creative thinkers, **3** Reflective learners, **5** Self-managers

2 a) Factors to consider in relation to the increased photocopying/printing charges include: the comparative prices charged by other schools/colleges, how often there is a price rise, whether any printing or photocopying at all can be done without charge, whether there are any concessions for special tasks or assignments, the availability of class sets of books/popular library books for loan (which reduces the need for photocopying).

b) i) An earlier start will be more likely to negatively affect those who live further away and who are reliant on public transport, particularly in rural areas. The earlier finish will benefit anyone who has a part-time job that starts on a Friday afternoon or who has after-college commitments, such as looking after younger sisters or brothers.

   ii) The scope for compromise would depend on whether there are any classes between 11 am and 2 pm on a Friday, whether tutors had any flexibility and whether the new 9 am – 11 am class could be moved to another time or day.

c) One strategy would be to allow discussion for a set time, ensure everyone has spoken, then put the issue to a vote. The leader should prompt suggestions from quieter members by asking people individually what they think.

Literacy skills action points (page 89)

2 a) The statement reads as if it is acceptable to either charge it or dispose of it in fire.
   b) Do not connect this battery improperly. Do not recharge it and do not dispose of it in fire.

3 Anyone who wishes to write books or reports, whether short or long, should try to use English grammatically. Obviously there is a need for correct spelling, too. Punctuation should also not be neglected.

Frequently, people confuse words with different meanings when they are writing, especially when these sound identical or very similar, even when they must not be spelled in the same way. The key to succeeding is due care, a lack of which leads to misspellings that might otherwise have been avoided. Spellcheckers do not find all mistakes.

Despite all the pitfalls, however, with practice, patience and the right attitude, anyone can soon become a great writer and speaker, like me.

4 Possible answers.

a) Stepping backwards and crossing arms across the chest might indicate that your manager is creating a barrier between you and himself. This may be because he is angry with you.

b) Your friend may be feeling guilty about what she did at the weekend, or not confident that you will approve of what she tells you.

c) Your tutor might be frustrated as he has many things to do and so wants the tutorial to finish quickly.

d) Your friend might be anxious about the next assignment or about the time she has to complete it.

Numeracy action points (page 92)

3 a) £60 million

b) Sophie's argument is incorrect as £50,000 is an average, some contestants will win more, but many will win much less. The distribution of prize money is greater at lower amounts because more people win small amounts of money than large amounts – and only five contestants have won the top prize of £1 million.

4 a) 300

b) 150

c) 9/10ths, 90%

d) 225:100 (= 45:20) = 9:4

e) 225:50 = 9:2

f) 600

g) £1530

Accessing website links

Links to various websites are referred to throughout this BTEC Level 3 National Study Skills Guide. To ensure that these links are up to date, that they work and that the sites aren't inadvertently linked to any material that could be considered offensive, we have made the links available on our website: www.pearsonhotlinks.co.uk. When you visit the site, search for either the title BTEC Level 3 National Study Skills Guide in Art and Design or ISBN 9781846905643. From here you can gain access to the website links and information on how they can be used to help you with your studies.

Useful terms

Accreditation of Prior Learning (APL)
Some of your previous achievements and experiences may be able to be used to count towards your qualification.

Apprenticeships
Schemes that enable you to work and earn money at the same time as you gain further qualifications (an NVQ award and a technical certificate) and improve your functional skills. Apprentices learn work-based skills relevant to their job role and their chosen industry. See page 96 for how you can access a website to find out more.

Assessment methods
Techniques used to check that your work demonstrates the learning and understanding required for your qualification, such as assignments, case studies and practical tasks.

Assessor
An assessor is the tutor who marks or assesses your work.

Assignment
A complex task or mini-project set to meet specific grading criteria and learning outcomes.

Awarding body
An organisation responsible for devising, assessing and issuing qualifications. The awarding body for all BTEC qualifications is Edexcel.

Credit value
The number of credits attached to your BTEC course. The credit value increases in relation to the length of time you need to complete the course, from 30 credits for a BTEC Level 3 Certificate, 60 credits for a Subsidiary Diploma, 120 credits for a Diploma, up to 180 credits for an Extended Diploma.

Degrees
Higher education qualifications offered by universities and colleges. Foundation degrees take two years to complete; honours degrees may take three years or longer.

Department for Business Innovation and Skills (BIS)
BIS is responsible for further and higher education and skills training, as well as functions related to trade and industry. See page 96 for how you can access a website to find out more.

Department for Education
The Department for Education is responsible for schools and education, as well as children's services. See page 96 for how you can access a website to find out more.

Distance learning
When you learn and/or study for a qualification at home or at work. You communicate with your tutor and/or the centre that organises the course by post, by telephone or electronically.

Educational Maintenance Award (EMA)
An EMA is a means-tested award that provides eligible learners under 19 who are studying a full-time course at school or college with a cash sum of money every week. See page 96 for how you can access a website to find out more.

External verification
Formal checking of the programme by an Edexcel representative that focuses on sampling various assignments to check content, accurate assessment and grading.

Forbidden combinations
There are some qualifications that cannot be taken simultaneously because their content is too similar.

Functional skills
Practical skills in English, maths and ICT that enable people to work confidently, effectively and independently. Level 2 Functional Skills are mapped to the units of BTEC Level 3 National qualifications. They aren't compulsory to achieve on the course, but are of great use.

Grade boundaries
Pre-set points that determine whether you will achieve a pass, merit or distinction as the overall final grade(s) for your qualification.

Grading criteria
The specific evidence you have to demonstrate to obtain a particular grade in the unit.

Grading domains

The main areas of learning that support the learning outcomes. On a BTEC Level 3 National course these are: application of knowledge and understanding; development of practical and technical skills; personal development for occupational roles; application of PLTS and functional skills.

Grading grid

The table in each unit of your qualification specification that sets out what you have to show you can do.

Higher education (HE)

Post-secondary and post-further education, usually provided by universities and colleges.

Higher-level skills

These are skills such as evaluating or critically assessing information. They are more difficult than lower-level skills such as writing a description or making a list. You must be able to demonstrate higher-level skills to achieve a distinction.

Indicative reading

Recommended books and journals whose content is both suitable and relevant for the BTEC unit studied.

Induction

A short programme of events at the start of a course designed to give you essential information and introduce you to your fellow learners and tutors, so that you can settle down as quickly and easily as possible.

Internal verification

The quality checks carried out by nominated tutors at your school or college to ensure that all assignments are at the right level and cover appropriate learning outcomes and grading criteria, and that all assessors are marking work consistently and to the same standard.

Investors in People (IiP)

A national quality standard that sets a level of good practice for training and developing of people within a business. Participating organisations must demonstrate commitment to achieving the standard.

Learning outcomes

The knowledge and skills you must demonstrate to show that you have effectively learned a unit.

Learning support

Additional help that is available to all learners in a school or college who have learning difficulties or other special needs.

Levels of study

The depth, breadth and complexity of knowledge, understanding and skills required to achieve a qualification, which also determine its level. Level 2 equates to GCSE level and Level 3 equates to A-level. As you successfully achieve one level, you can then progress to the next. BTEC qualifications are offered at Entry Level, then Levels 1, 2, 3, 4 and 5.

Local Education Authority (LEA)

The local government body responsible for providing education for all learners of compulsory school age. The LEA is also responsible for managing the education budget for 16–19-year-old learners in its area.

Mandatory units

These are units that all learners must complete to gain a qualification, in this case a BTEC Level 3 National. Some BTEC qualifications have an over-arching title, eg Construction, but within Construction you can choose different pathways. Your chosen pathway may have additional mandatory units specific to that pathway.

Mentor

A more experienced person who will guide you and counsel you if you have a problem or difficulty.

Mode of delivery

The way in which a qualification is offered to learners, for example part-time, full-time, as a short course or by distance learning.

National Occupational Standard (NOS)

Statements of the skills, knowledge and understanding you need to develop in order to be competent at a particular job.

National Vocational Qualification (NVQ)

Qualifications that concentrate on the practical skills and knowledge required to do a job competently. They are usually assessed in the workplace and range from Level 1 (the lowest) to Level 5 (the highest).

Nested qualifications

Qualifications that have 'common' units, so that learners can easily progress from one to another by adding on more units

Ofqual
The public body responsible for regulating qualifications, exams and tests in England.

Optional units
Units on your course from which you may be able to make a choice. They help you specialise your skills, knowledge and understanding, and may help progression into work or further education.

Pathway
All BTEC Level 3 National qualifications comprise a small number of mandatory units and a larger number of optional units. These units are grouped into different combinations to provide alternative pathways to achieving the qualification. These pathways are usually linked to different career preferences.

Peer review
This involves feedback on your performance by your peers (members of your team or class group.) You will also be given an opportunity to review their performance.

Plagiarism
The practice of copying someone else's work or work from any other sources (eg the internet), and passing it off as your own. This practice is strictly forbidden on all courses.

Personal, learning and thinking skills (PLTS)
The skills, personal qualities and behaviour that improve your ability to work independently. Developing these skills makes you more effective and confident at work. Opportunities for developing these skills are a feature of all BTEC Level 3 National courses. These skills aren't compulsory to achieve on the course, but are of great use to you.

Portfolio
A collection of work compiled by a learner, usually as evidence of learning, to present to an assessor.

Procrastinator
Someone who is forever putting off or delaying work, either because they are lazy or because they have poor organisational skills.

Professional body
An organisation that exists to promote or support a particular profession, for example the Royal Institute of British Architects (RIBA).

Professional development and training
This involves undertaking activities relevant to your job to increase and/or update your knowledge and skills.

Project
A project is a comprehensive piece of work, which normally involves original research and investigation by an individual or by a team. The findings and results may be presented in writing and summarised as a presentation.

Qualifications and Credit Framework (QCF)
The QCF is a framework for recognising skills and qualifications. It does this by awarding credit for qualifications and units so that they are easier to measure and compare. All BTEC Level 3 National qualifications are part of the QCF.

Qualifications and Curriculum Development Agency (QCDA)
The QCDA is responsible for maintaining and developing the national curriculum, delivering assessments, tests and examinations, and reforming qualifications.

Quality assurance
In education, this is the process of continually checking that a course of study is meeting the specific requirements set down by the awarding body.

Sector Skills Councils (SSCs)
The 25 employer-led, independent organisations responsible for improving workforce skills in the UK by identifying skill gaps and improving learning in the workplace. Each council covers a different type of industry.

Semester
Many universities and colleges divide their academic year into two halves or semesters, one from September to January and one from February to July.

Seminar
A learning event involving a group of learners and a tutor, which may be learner-led, and may follow research into a topic that has been introduced at an earlier stage.

Study buddy
A person in your group or class who takes notes for you and keeps you informed of important developments if you are absent. You do the same for them in return.

Time-constrained assignment

An assessment you must complete within a fixed time limit.

Tutorial

An individual or small group meeting with your tutor at which you can discuss your current work and other more general course issues. At an individual tutorial, your progress on the course will be discussed and you can raise any concerns or personal worries you may have.

The University and Colleges Admissions Service (UCAS)

UCAS (pronounced 'you-cass') is the central organisation that processes all applications for higher education (HE) courses.

UCAS points

The number of points allocated by UCAS for the qualifications you have obtained. Higher education institutions specify how many points you need to be accepted on the courses they offer. See page 96 for how you can access a website to find out more.

Unit abstract

The summary at the start of each BTEC unit that tells you what the unit is about.

Unit content

Details about the topics covered by the unit and the knowledge and skills you need to complete it.

Unit points

The number of points you gain when you complete a unit. These will depend on the grade you achieve (pass, merit or distinction).

Vocational qualification

Designed to develop knowledge and understanding relevant to a chosen area of work.

Work experience

Time you spend on an employer's premises when you learn about the enterprise, carry out work-based tasks, and develop skills and knowledge.

Please note that all information given within these useful terms was correct at the time of going to print.